SYRIA, LEBANON, AND JORDAN

MIDDLE EAST
REGION IN TRANSITION

SYRIA, LEBANON, AND JORDAN

EDITED BY LAURA S. ETHEREDGE, ASSOCIATE EDITOR, MIDDLE EAST GEOGRAPHY

Britannica® Educational Publishing
IN ASSOCIATION WITH
ROSEN
EDUCATIONAL SERVICES

Published in 2011 by Britannica Educational Publishing
(a trademark of Encyclopædia Britannica, Inc.)
in association with Rosen Educational Services, LLC
29 East 21st Street, New York, NY 10010.

Distributed exclusively by Rosen Educational Services.
For a listing of additional Britannica Educational Publishing titles, call toll free (800) 237-9932.

First Edition

Britannica Educational Publishing
Michael I. Levy: Executive Editor
J.E. Luebering: Senior Manager
Marilyn L. Barton: Senior Coordinator, Production Control
Steven Bosco: Director, Editorial Technologies
Lisa S. Braucher: Senior Producer and Data Editor
Yvette Charboneau: Senior Copy Editor
Kathy Nakamura: Manager, Media Acquisition
Laura S. Etheredge: Associate Editor, Middle East Geography

Rosen Educational Services
Heather M. Moore Niver: Editor
Nelson Sá: Art Director
Cindy Reiman: Photography Manager
Matthew Cauli: Designer, Cover Design
Introduction by Shalini Saxena

Library of Congress Cataloging-in-Publication Data

Syria, Lebanon, and Jordan/edited by Laura S. Etheredge. — 1st ed.
p. cm. — (Middle East: region in transition)
"In association with Britannica Educational Publishing, Rosen Educational Services."
Includes bibliographical references and index.
ISBN 978-1-61530-329-8 (library binding)
1. Syria. 2. Lebanon. 3. Jordan. 4. Social change—Syria–History. 5. Social change—Lebanon—History. 6. Social change—Jordan—History. I. Etheredge, Laura.
DS93.S956 2011
956.9—dc22

2010027853

Manufactured in the United States of America

On the cover: Syria, Jordan, and Lebanon feature everything from wild rugged coasts to teeming metros, from modern skyscrapers to hallowed ancient ruins. (Clockwise, from top left: Pigeon Rocks and city of Beirut, Lebanon; ancient city of Petra, Jordan; Amman, Jordan; Palmyra ruins, Syria.) *Shutterstock.com*

On pages 1, 18, 27, 32, 39, 85, 95, 104, 111, 117, 160, 173, 181, 186, 190, 211, 213, 219: The water-conservative camel proves to be a useful animal to humans on the steppes. *Awad Awad AFP/Getty Images*

CONTENTS

33

34

48

78

90

97

109

111

117

149

162

169

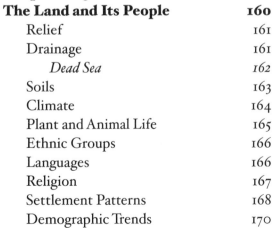

184

188

192

195

INTRODUCTION

Positioned at a crossroads between the Mediterranean and the Middle East, the countries of Syria, Lebanon, and Jordan have absorbed a pastiche of influences, including Semitic, Greek, Roman, and Turkish elements, some of which are still evident within the unique traditions that define each country. Although their long histories have often intertwined, each country has a singular story to tell. This volume chronicles the narratives that both bind these countries together and set them apart.

Geographically and climatically, Syria, Lebanon, and Jordan have much in common. Though each naturally differs in many respects as well, their proximity to one another has yielded shared topographies and landscapes. The three countries are also linked ethnically: Arabs constitute the majority in each country, and Arabic is the predominant language throughout the region. Various ethnic minorities are present in each country as well, some of which have been assimilated or Arabized, and some of which continue to practice distinct traditions and speak languages other than Arabic. Armenian communities thrive in all three countries, for example, while Syria and Lebanon are home to Kurdish populations. Turkmen and other groups are also variously distributed throughout the countries.

As the most widely practiced religion in the region, Islam has helped shape the history and culture of all three countries. In Syria and Jordan, Sunni Muslims form a clear majority of the population. The religious composition of Lebanon is much more complex and includes a Muslim population divided between Shīʿites and Sunnis, as well

Columns of salt rising from the extremely saline waters of the Dead Sea.
Peter Carmichael/ASPECT

as a variety of Christian denominations. While Christians are also present in Syria and Jordan, they are most visibly represented in Lebanon.

Despite some similarities shared by these countries, however, their respective historical trajectories reveal distinct cultures whose relations with each other and the surrounding region have alternately meant peace and instability in each.

Syria is the largest of the three countries, and, along with Lebanon, is one of the countries traditionally considered part of the Levant. Through World War I, "Syria" encompassed parts of Lebanon, Transjordan, and Palestine, in addition to what is present-day Syria. Even today, the fates of Syria's neighbours are closely tied to its policies and actions.

Rural life in Syria has mainly developed around agricultural activity. Meanwhile, urban centres continuously draw workers away from pastoral life toward the promise of commercial opportunities in large cities like Aleppo and Damascus, the country's capital. Today, Syria's urban and rural populations are of almost equal size.

Syria is a socialist state, and the government exercises control over the country's economy. Although Syria's principal export is petroleum, production peaked in the 1990s and has since been declining. The privatization of the tourism industry—which has flourished thanks to the wealth of cultural landmarks the country offers—has brought in a significant amount of revenue and stimulated economic growth during the 1990s. Among the features attracting tourists are the ruins at Palmyra and the Krak des Chevaliers Crusader fortress, each a testament to the complex cultural heritage that defines the character of the country.

With the socialist Baʿth party at the helm, Syria has achieved a measure of political stability. The party's influence is extensive, and although elections are held, they are not typically free. Additionally, while the constitution guarantees certain basic rights like freedom of expression, they are not always observed in practice. The country's legal system is based on tenets of Islamic law and, to a lesser extent, on French civil code.

The earliest evidence of life in Syria dates back to the Middle Paleolithic Period. Metallurgy becomes apparent in the region after the mid-4th millennium BCE, and cities developed shortly thereafter. From the 13th century BCE onward, power in Syria passed through many hands, including the Aramaeans, Assyrians, Babylonians, Persians, and—in the middle of the 4th century BCE—the Greeks. Syria later fell to the Romans, but Greek ways of life and ideas were already firmly entrenched in Syrian culture. Cultural advancements continued well after Greek power declined, and new traditions were often co-opted into Syrian habitus.

In the 7th century CE, Syria fell to the Arabs during the Islamic conquests. The Umayyad dynasty, which ruled for nearly a century, established its seat of power in Damascus and became instrumental in extending the influence of Islam and nourishing the arts and sciences throughout Syria. After the fall of the Umayyads, Syria was subject to the rule first of the Abbasids and then, over the centuries, to a series of local and foreign successors.

In the 16th century, Syria fell to the Ottomans and commenced a 400-year period under their generally continuous rule. After World War I, power passed from the Ottomans to the French, whose mandate over the region was approved by the League of Nations in 1922. Tensions between Syrians who demanded independence and the French prompted British involvement to aid the French cause. After years of disagreement, Syria was finally granted independence in 1946.

As with many other newly created republics, stability was tenuous in the early years of Syria's independence. After a brief venture conjoined with Egypt as the United Arab Republic, Syria regained its sovereignty and subsequently ushered in the era of Ba'thist rule. Ḥafiz al-Assad, a member of the country's 'Alawite minority, seized power and was sworn in as president in 1971. Assad's steady—though often oppressive—rule brought a measure of stability to the country despite Syrian involvement in a number of regional conflicts. Following Assad's death in 2000, his son, Bashar al-Assad, assumed power. Although the younger Assad implemented some degree of economic and social change in Syria, he did not enact a dramatic shift away from his father's policies. Even as it inches toward greater liberalization in certain spheres, Syria continues to be embroiled in international controversy and tumultuous relationships with many of its neighbours.

Lebanon, inhabited since the Paleolithic Period, has historically welcomed settlers, visitors, and traders of various ethnicities and religious persuasions. Like Syria, Lebanon boasts vestiges of a rich and ancient past with its numerous cultural sites. However, the country has also been vulnerable to intense conflict, with the civil war of 1975–1990 being the most damaging in its recent history. The destruction it wrought has penetrated almost every level of Lebanese society and continues to demonstrate its legacy.

In the postwar era, reconstruction projects helped Lebanon regain some of its earlier economic confidence. Prosperity was generally concentrated in the hands of a few Lebanese, however, while many more continued to live below the poverty line. Lacking much in the way of natural resources, the country had traditionally relied on its status as a financial hub, a centre of trade, and an attractive tourist destination. Although the economy as a whole suffered as a result of the civil war, the damage to the service sector was especially profound.

Lebanon is a multiparty republic with a parliamentary system of government. Power is vested in a president, prime minister, and unicameral legislature, the National Assembly, whose composition mirrors the heterogeneity of the populace. A de facto understanding has produced a system where the president is always a Maronite Christian, the prime minister a Sunni, and the speaker of the National Assembly a Shīʿite. Regional governorates oversee local matters, and the justice system is largely modeled on the French system of law.

The Phoenician traders of ancient Lebanon were vital to the development of the region. With colonies flourishing along the coast of the Levant by the 2nd millennium BCE and others soon established around the Mediterranean, the Phoenicians were able to access numerous cultural and natural resources. After becoming subject in turn to Assyrian, Babylonian, and Persian rule, the region fell to the Greeks and then the Romans in the 4th and 1st centuries BCE, respectively.

In the 7th century CE, Lebanon's population began increasingly to resemble its present-day composition with a substantial community of Maronite Christians and a growing Muslim population. The region came under the sway of the Umayyad dynasty in the 7th and 8th centuries, with portions of Lebanon being governed as part of the Damascus district. After periods of rule by independent Egyptian dynasties as well as the Crusaders, Ayyūbids, and Mamlūks, the region came under Ottoman rule in the 16th century.

In 1860, religious conflict between the Maronites and Druze occasioned French intervention on behalf of the Maronites and anticipated the eventual replacement of

Ottoman rule with French mandate in the early 1920s. Under the French, conflict between the groups ebbed and infrastructure and education improved throughout the country. Soon, however, Lebanese contingents began agitating for sovereignty, and Lebanon achieved full independence in 1946.

Although confessional conflict persisted after independence, Lebanon was soon able to achieve a measure of stability and economic growth. Religious conflict was increasingly compounded by growing socioeconomic tensions, however, and sparked civil war in 1975. Foreign intervention by Syria and Israel helped to perpetuate the violence until 1990, when Syrian troops ousted Maronite leader Michel Aoun, head of the remnant of the Lebanese Army and one of two competing claimants to the premiership. While the civil war was technically ended, the conflict it represented was transferred into the political realm. One group competing for influence was Hezbollah, a militant Islamic group established during the civil war. The 2006 war between the Hezbollah and Israel, which caused extensive further damage to Lebanese infrastructure, is just one example of the many problems that threaten continued Lebanese peace into the 21st century.

Like its neighbours, Jordan has had to navigate complex international situations while maintaining a delicate peace on the domestic front. Although Jordan has reached peace with Israel and has a good relationship with the West, it has become embroiled in various conflicts by virtue of its location and its especially large Palestinian population, a distinctive feature that gives it a prominent stake in the resolution of the Arab-Israeli conflict.

More than four-fifths of Jordan's population resides in one of its major cities, including its capital, Amman. The remaining rural population includes those settled in villages, as well as the country's Bedouin tribes. The Jordanian economy is largely dependent on the country's service sector, which is the most important contributor in terms of both value and employment.

Jordan is a constitutional monarchy with a parliamentary form of government, the executive, legislative, and judicial branches of which are all subject to the king's authority. Local administration occurs in the form of governorates. The judiciary consists of three types of courts, including Sharīʿah (Islamic law) courts (and other religious courts, for non-Muslims) that handle issues related to personal status.

Jordan possesses a wealth of artifacts and ruins, such as those at Petra, that are significant to its pre-Islamic heritage. Others, such as the country's famed desert castles, recall its early Islamic history. Although Jordan's Arab and Muslim character continues to define much in the way of its daily life, the country as a whole has also generally welcomed international influences and culture.

Jordan as a state is comparatively young, but the ancient land it occupies has witnessed centuries of events that bear a central role in many biblical accounts. Following Muslim conquest in the 7th century, the area that would later form modern Jordan—like much of the region—came under Umayyad rule. When the Abbasids seized the caliphate in the mid-8th century, the caliphal capital was moved eastward from neighbouring Damascus to Baghdad, and the region declined into something of a backwater.

In 1922, Ottoman rule in Jordan—which had begun in the 16th century—was effectively replaced with British rule when the League of Nations confirmed the British mandate over a region that included Transjordan (as it was called until 1949). Transjordan gained full independence in 1946 but became enmeshed in the first Arab-Israeli war soon thereafter. It acquired the West Bank and East Jerusalem in 1949, both of which it annexed the following year; this decision dramatically altered the structure of the country's population to include almost as many Palestinians as Jordanians. Relations with Israel consumed a large part of Jordan's attention under the rule of King Ḥussein, who was crowned in 1953.

In the next Arab-Israeli war in 1967, Jordan lost the West Bank and East Jerusalem to Israel. This not only generated hundreds of thousands of Palestinian refugees—so creating severe economic problems in the country—but spurred the rise of the Palestinian Liberation Organization (PLO) as a representative of the Palestinian people. Tension between the PLO and the Jordanian state whose sovereignty it threatened eventually led to the expulsion of the PLO by force from Jordan in 1970–71. Although the West Bank and East Jerusalem had been lost, the fate of the Palestinians (including the numerous refugees who remained in Jordan) continued to be a central concern for Jordan into the 21st century, and Jordan remained an active participant in the Arab-Israeli peace process.

Syria, Lebanon, and Jordan have been susceptible to periods of both domestic and international turmoil over the centuries. As they continue to shape their relationships with one another and the world, their participation in peace initiatives both at home and abroad will have significant implications for the progress of Middle East peace and the delicate coexistence that would ensure its sustainability.

Syria: The Land and Its People

CHAPTER 1

Syria is a country located on the east coast of the Mediterranean Sea. Its area, which includes territory in the Golan Heights that has been occupied by Israel since 1967, does not coincide with ancient Syria, which was the strip of fertile land lying between the eastern Mediterranean coast and the desert of northern Arabia. Modern Syria is bounded by Turkey to the north, Iraq to the east and southeast, Jordan to the south, and Lebanon and Israel to the southwest.

The Syrian people evolved from several origins over a long period of time. The Greek and Roman ethnic influence was negligible in comparison with that of the Semitic peoples of Arabia and Mesopotamia—Aramaeans, Assyrians, Chaldeans, and Canaanites. Later the Turks,

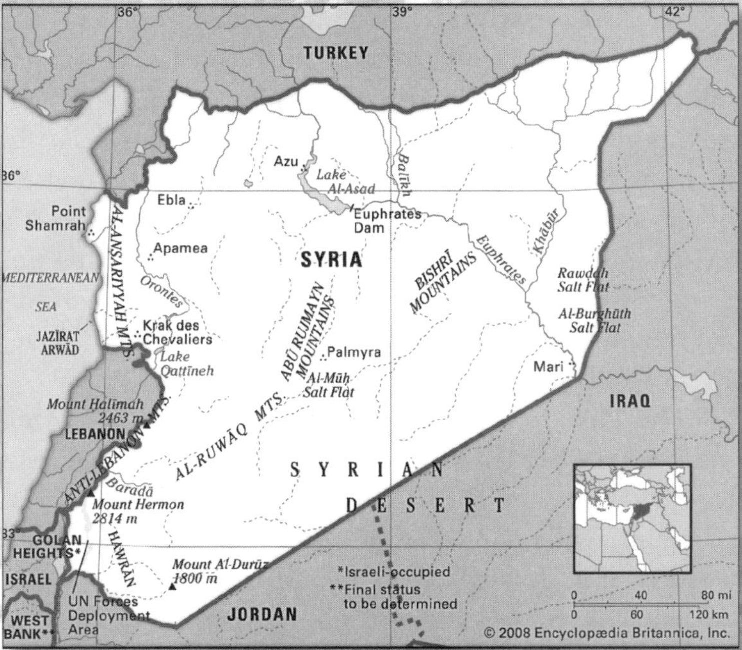

With a rather scant coastline along the Mediterranean Sea, Syria shares borders with Turkey, Iraq, Jordan, Israel, and Lebanon.

like the Greeks and Romans before them, influenced political and economic structures but failed to produce any noticeable change in the dominant Arab character of the Syrian people.

RELIEF

Syria has a relatively short coastline, which stretches for about 110 miles (180 kilometres) along the Mediterranean Sea between the countries of Turkey and Lebanon. Sandy bays dent the shore, alternating with rocky headlands and low cliffs. North of Ṭarṭūs, the narrow coastal strip is interrupted by spurs of the northwestern Al-Anṣariyyah Mountains immediately to the east. It then widens into the ʿAkkār Plain, which continues south across the Lebanon border.

The Al-Anṣariyyah mountain range borders the coastal plain and runs from north to south. The mountains have an average width of 20 miles (32 km), and their average height declines from 3,000 feet (900 metres) in the north to 2,000 feet in the south. Their highest point, at 5,125 feet (1,562 m), is situated east of Latakia (Al-Lādhiqiyyah). Directly to the east of the mountains is the Ghāb Depression, a 40-mile (64-km) longitudinal trench that contains the valley of the Orontes River (Nahr Al-ʿĀṣī).

The Anti-Lebanon Mountains (Al-Jabal al-Sharqī) mark Syria's border with Lebanon. The main ridge rises to a maximum height of 8,625 feet (2,629 metres) near Al-Nabk, while the mean height is between 6,000 and 7,000 feet (1,800 to 2,100 m). Mount Hermon (Jabal Al-Shaykh), Syria's highest point, rises to 9,232 feet (2,814 m).

Smaller mountains are scattered about the country. Among these are Mount Al-Durūz, which rises to an

Mount Hermon

Mount Hermon (Arabic: Jabal Al-Shaykh) is a snowcapped ridge on the Lebanon-Syria border west of Damascus. It rises to 9,232 feet (2,814 metres) and is sometimes considered the southernmost extension of the Anti-Lebanon range. At its foot rise the two major sources of the Jordan River. Hermon has also been known historically as Sirion and Senir. A sacred landmark in Hittite, Palestinian, and Roman times, it represented the northwestern limit of Israelite conquest under Moses and Joshua. On its slopes are temples with Greek inscriptions dating from about 200 CE.

Since the June (Six-Day) War of 1967, about 40 square miles (100 square km) of Mount Hermon's southern and western slopes have been part of the Israeli-administered Golan Heights. These areas have been developed for recreational use, especially skiing.

elevation of some 5,900 feet (1,800 m) in the extreme south, and the Abū Rujmayn and Bishrī mountains, which stretch northeastward across the central part of the country.

The undulating plains occupying the rest of the country are known as the Syrian Desert. In general their elevation lies between 980 and 1,640 feet (300 and 500 m); they are seldom less than 820 feet (250 m) above sea level. The area is not a sand desert but comprises rock and gravel steppe. A mountainous region in the south-central area is known as Al-Ḥamād.

DRAINAGE

The Euphrates River is the most important water source and the only navigable river in Syria. It originates in Turkey and flows southeastward across the eastern part of Syria. The Euphrates Dam, constructed on the river at

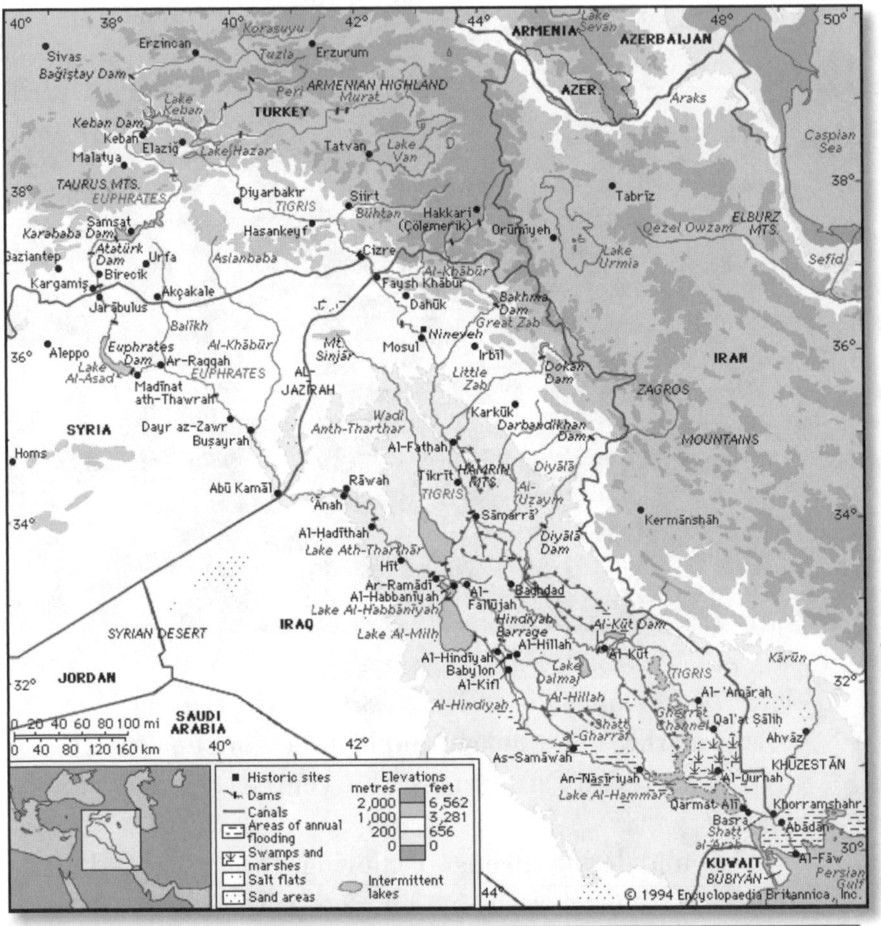

The Tigris and Euphrates river basin and its drainage network.

Ṭabaqah, was completed in 1973, and the reservoir behind the dam, Lake Al-Assad, began to fill thereafter.

The Orontes is the principal river of the mountainous region. It rises in Lebanon, flows northward through the mountains and the Ghāb Depression, and enters the Mediterranean near Antioch (Hatay), Turkey. The Yarmūk River, a tributary of the Jordan River, drains the Jabal Al-Durūz and Ḥawrān regions and forms part of the border with Jordan in the southwest.

Orontes River

The Orontes River (Arabic: Nahr Al-ʿĀṣī), located in southwestern Asia, drains a large part of the northern Levant into the Mediterranean Sea. From its source in the Bekaa Valley of central Lebanon, the river flows northward between the parallel ranges of the Lebanon and Anti-Lebanon Mountains into Syria, where it has been dammed to form Lake Qaṭṭīnah. Northwest of Ḥamāh the Orontes crosses the fertile Ghāb Depression and enters Turkey, where it bends westward and empties into the sea near Samandağı. Largely unnavigable for most of its 250-mile (400-km) length, it is nonetheless an important source of irrigation water, especially between Ḥimṣ and Ḥamāh. Major tributaries of the Orontes include the Karasu and ʿAfrīn rivers. Ḥimṣ, Ḥamāh, and the ancient Greek city of Antioch (Hatay, Turkey) are the largest riparian settlements.

Scattered lakes are found in Syria. The largest is Al-Jabbūl, a seasonal saline lake that permanently covers a minimum area of about 60 square miles (155 square km) southeast of Aleppo. Other major salt lakes are Jayrūd to the northeast of Damascus and Khātūniyyah to the northeast of Al-Ḥasakah. Lake Muzayrīb, a small body of fresh water, is located northwest of Darʿā. The larger Lake Qaṭṭīnah (Lake Ḥimṣ), a reservoir, is west of Ḥimṣ (Homs).

Most of the country's drainage flows underground. On the surface, impervious rocks—consisting of clay, marl (clay, sand, or silt), and greensand—cover a relatively small area. Porous rocks cover about half of the country and are mainly sandstone or chalk. Highly porous rocks consist of basalt and limestone. Water penetrates the porous rocks, forming underground springs, rivers, or subterranean water sheets close to the surface. Although the springs are profuse, the water sheets are quickly exhausted and may turn saline in areas of low precipitation.

SOILS

Because of aridity, vegetation plays only a secondary role in soil composition. With the exception of the black soil in the northeastern region of Al-Jazīrah, soils are deficient in phosphorus and organic matter. The most common soils are various clays and loams (mixtures of clay, sand, and silt). Some are calcareous (chalky), whereas others—especially in the area of the Euphrates Valley—contain gypsum. Alluvial soils occur mainly in the valleys of the Euphrates and its tributaries and in the Ghāb Depression.

CLIMATE

The coast and the western mountains have a Mediterranean climate with a long dry season from May to October. In the extreme northwest there is some light summer rain. On the coast summers are hot, with mean daily maximum temperatures in the low to mid-80s °F (upper 20s °C), while the mild winters have daily mean minimum temperatures reaching the low 50s °F (low 10s °C). Only above about 5,000 feet (1,500 metres) are the summers relatively cool. Inland the climate becomes arid, with colder winters and hotter summers. Maximum temperatures in Damascus and Aleppo average in the 90s °F (mid-30s °C) in summer, while temperatures reach average lows in the mid-30s to low 40s °F (1 to 4 °C) in winter. In the desert, at Tadmur (Palmyra) and Dayr al-Zawr, maximum temperatures in the summer reach averages in the upper 90s to low 100s °F (upper 30s to low 40s °C), with extremes in the 110s °F (mid- to upper 40s °C). Snow may occur in winter away from the coast, and frosts are common.

The coast and western mountains receive 30 to 40 inches (760 to 1000 mm) of precipitation annually. Annual precipitation decreases rapidly eastward: the steppe receives 10 to 20 inches (250 to 500 mm), Mount Al-Durūz receives more than 8 inches (200 mm), and the desert area of Al-Ḥamād receives less than 5 inches (130 mm). Precipitation is variable from year to year, particularly in the spring and autumn months.

In winter the prevailing winds blow from the east, the north, and the west. In summer the prevailing winds are either northerly or westerly. During the summer the coastal region is subject to westerly winds during the day and easterly ones at night. Once or twice a year sand-bearing winds known as the khamsin raise a wall of dust some 5,000 feet (1,500 m) high, which darkens the sky.

Plant and Animal Life

Yew, lime, and fir trees grow on the mountain slopes and date palms are found in the Euphrates valley. In both coastal and inland regions, plants include grains, olive trees, grapevines, apricot trees, oaks, and poplars. Lemon and orange trees grow along the coast. Garigue, a degenerate Mediterranean scrub, and maquis, a thick scrubby underbrush, cover many slopes.

Forests make up only a very small percentage of the country's total area and are primarily found in the mountains, especially in the Al-Anṣariyyah Mountains. Glossy-leaved and thorny drought-resistant shrubs such as myrtle, boxwood, turpentine, broom, arbutus, and wild olive abound to the south. Excessive exploitation of the forests for their wood has largely turned them into scrub. A reforestation project has been undertaken in the mountains north of Latakia, however, and some forests are protected by the government. Commercially important forest plants include sumac, which is used as a spice, wild pistachio, which is important for its oil-rich fruit, laurel, which is used in the production of cosmetics, and mulberry, whose leaves are fed to silkworms. Pine tree branches are used for smoking tobacco leaves. Other useful plants are winter vegetables such as *khubbayzah*, a kind of spinach; *'akkūb*, a flowering plant; and truffles. Licorice is widely exploited for its root, which is used in the pharmaceutical industry.

The steppe is characterized by the absence of natural tree cover, except for some sparsely distributed hawthorns. All other trees—such as those in the orchards of Damascus and Aleppo and along the banks of the Orontes and Euphrates rivers—are cultivated.

For a brief period before June, the land is covered with a variety of flowering and grassy plants. Under the implacable sun of June, however, the plants soon wither, casting off their seeds onto the dry ground.

Wild animal life is sparse. Wolves, hyenas, foxes, badgers, wild boar, and jackals can still be found in remote areas. Deer, bears, squirrels, and such small carnivores as martens and polecats are also found, while desert animals include gazelles and jerboas (nocturnal jumping rodents). Vipers, lizards, and chameleons are common in the desert. Eagles, buzzards, kites, and falcons frequent the mountains. Harmful insects include mosquitoes, sandflies, grasshoppers, and occasionally locusts.

The mule is the beast of burden in the mountains, and the camel on the steppe. Other domesticated animals include horses, donkeys, cattle, sheep, goats, and chickens. Bees also are kept.

ETHNIC AND LINGUISTIC GROUPS

There is a rough correspondence between ethnic and linguistic groupings, although some ethnic groups have been partially assimilated by the Arab majority, which includes the country's Bedouin population. A Kurdish minority also resides in Syria. Much of the Kurdish population is Arabic-speaking and largely resides in the country's northeast. The country's Armenian population may be divided into two groups—the early settlers, who have been more or less Arabized, and the later immigrants, who arrived after World War I and retained their identity and language. The Turkmen intermingle freely with the Kurds and Arabs, but they have lost none of their ethnic identity in some northern villages. Syriac-speaking Assyrians who immigrated to Syria from Iraq as refugees in the 1930s quickly assimilated, owing to intermarriage and migration to the cities.

The great majority of the population speaks Arabic. Other languages spoken in Syria include Kurdish, spoken in the extreme northeast and northwest; Armenian, spoken in Aleppo and other major cities; and Turkish, spoken in villages east of the Euphrates and along the border with Turkey. Adyghian, a Kabardian (Circassian) language, is also spoken by a minority of the population. English and French are understood, particularly in urban centres and among the educated.

RELIGION

Four-fifths of the population is Muslim. Sunni Muslims account for about three-fourths of Syria's Muslim population and are in the majority everywhere in the country except in the southern Al-Suwaydā' *muḥāfaẓah* (governorate) and the Latakia governorate in the north. The ʿAlawites (a Shīʿite subsect) are the next largest group, and most live in the Latakia governorate or in the governorates of Ḥimṣ and Ḥamāh. Most of the country's Druze population lives in Al-Suwaydā' governorate, and the rest in Damascus, Aleppo, and Al-Qunayṭirah.

Christians constitute almost one-tenth of the Syrian population. They are divided into several churches, which include Greek Orthodox, Greek Catholic, Syrian Orthodox, Armenian Catholic, Armenian Apostolic (Orthodox), Syrian Catholic, Maronite, Protestant, Nestorian, Latin, and Chaldean. There is also a small Jewish population, the remainder of what once had been a flourishing community before being subjected to limitations on travel, employment, and other restrictions imposed by the Syrian government. Following international pressure on Syria to allow them to leave the country, much of the Jewish population chose to emigrate in the late 20th century; many chose to settle in New York City.

SETTLEMENT PATTERNS

Syria consists of four traditional regions: the coastal strip, the mountains, the cultivated steppe, and the desert steppe. On the coast the fertile alluvial plains are intensively cultivated in both summer and winter. The region is the site of Syria's two principal ports of Latakia and Ṭarṭūs.

Courtyard of the Great Mosque of Aleppo, Syria. Sam Abboud—FPG

The area around the northwestern Al-Anṣariyyah Mountains is the only densely forested region. It is the ancient stronghold of the ʿAlawites, who form a sect of Shīʿite Islam. The economic resources of the mountains are too meagre to

'Alawite

'Alawites are members of a minority sect of Shīʿite Muslims living chiefly in Syria. Considered by many Muslims to be heretics, the present-day 'Alawites obtained a legal decision about their status as Muslims from the Lebanese leader of the Ithnā 'Asharī (Twelver) sect of Shīʿite Islam. The 'Alawite sect has become politically dominant in Syria, particularly since 1971, when Ḥafiz al-Assad, an 'Alawite, was elected president of the country. The sect is predominant in the Latakia region of Syria, and it extends north to Antioch, in Turkey. Many 'Alawites also live around or in Ḥimṣ and Ḥamāh. They are second in number within Syria to the Sunni sect, which makes up about three-fourths of the Muslim population of mostly Muslim Syria.

The basic doctrine of 'Alawite faith is the deification of 'Alī. He is one member of a trinity corresponding roughly to the Christian Father, Son, and Holy Spirit. 'Alawites interpret the Pillars of Islam (the five duties required of every Muslim) as symbols and thus do not practice the Islamic duties. They celebrate an eclectic group of holidays, some Islamic, some Christian, and many 'Alawite practices are secret. They consider themselves to be moderate Shīʿites, not much different from the Twelvers.

meet the needs of the ever-growing population, so there is migration to the Ghāb Depression and coastal towns.

The cultivated steppe region constitutes the principal wheat zone, and agriculture is intensively pursued along the banks of the rivers. Some of Syria's most important cities—Damascus, Aleppo, Ḥimṣ, Ḥamāh, and Al-Qāmishlī—are situated there.

The arid desert steppe country is the natural domain of the nomads and seminomads. Sheep graze until the beginning of summer, when water becomes scarce, after which the shepherds lead their flocks either westward into the cultivated steppe or to the hills. The area once contained oases that served as caravan towns on the trade route joining Mesopotamia and the Indian Ocean with the countries of the Mediterranean. The most famous of these towns is Palmyra (Tadmur), at the northern edge of the Syrian Desert. The most important feature of the region is the Euphrates River.

Rural Settlement

In areas of traditional rural settlement, the choice of a village site is usually determined by the availability of water. Some of the villages in the Al-Anṣariyyah Mountains, however, have given priority to the requirements of defense and fortification. Village dwellings stand close together, and village streets are extremely narrow. Usually, there is a small central common overlooked by a minaret (a tall tower attached to a mosque from which the populace is called to prayer). There are usually a few small shops containing articles manufactured in the cities or towns.

In rural areas, work takes place according to the seasonal rhythm of agriculture. Women generally share in much of the agricultural labour. Agricultural machinery, introduced on a large scale after World War II, caused unemployment and drove many villagers to the cities.

Attempts to restrict the Bedouin took place during Ottoman rule and were later taken up again by the French, who had initially encouraged Bedouin self-government. These efforts continued after Syrian independence in the 1940s, and in 1958 the land of the *bādiyah* (Syrian Desert)—which accounted for some four-fifths of Syrian territory—was nationalized, and tribal holdings were no longer recognized by the state. Pasturelands were ruined and vast quantities of sheep and camels were lost in the massive drought of 1958–61, which devastated many Syrian Bedouin. Many were forced to seek employment in the urban centres, and some did not return to their pastoral lifestyle after the drought was over. Others, however, became partners with urban merchants who sponsored the restocking of their flocks. With the activation of state-sponsored programs, pastoral activity was revived, albeit in a new form: subsidized fodder and government-drilled wells were used in the nourishment of the herds, migration became increasingly individualized, and pastoral endeavours grew more market-oriented.

Urban Settlement

Ten centuries of Greek and Roman rule left an urban mark still visible in the towns of Latakia, Tadmur, and Buṣrā al-Shām (ancient Bostra). The urban tradition of Islam appears in such cities as Damascus and Aleppo. The continuation of old commercial and religious interests enabled the cities to maintain their economic and cultural supremacy under the four centuries of Ottoman rule. Following a period of rapid urbanization in the 1950s and '60s, rural-to-urban migration abated somewhat. Nevertheless, disparities between rural and urban areas, albeit reduced on several fronts, persisted into the 21st century and contributed to Syrians' continued movement from rural to urban areas.

The national capital and second largest city in Syria is Damascus, situated in the southeast on the banks of the Baradā River. It is not only the national headquarters of government and the diplomatic community but also the main centre of education, culture, and industry. In addition, it serves as a marketing hub for central Syria and produces traditional handicraft products such as brocades, engraved wood, gold and silver ornaments, and carpets. It is well served by transport facilities and public utilities.

Aleppo, which is located between the Orontes and Euphrates rivers, is the country's largest city and a trade

Sheepherder with his flock on the outskirts of a village near Aleppo, Syria. Shostal Associates

and light-industry centre. The city is well served by roads and railroads and is surrounded by an area that specializes in the production of sheep for market in Damascus and other countries. The Mediterranean port of Latakia is surrounded by a rich agricultural region and contains some industry. Because of its seaside location, the city is a major tourist centre.

Ḥimṣ is located in the midst of a fertile plain east of the Orontes River. It is a hub of the country's road and railway systems. Ḥamāh, to the northeast of Ḥimṣ, is bisected by the Orontes River. It contains irrigated orchards and is an agricultural trade centre. There is also some light industry.

In 1982 the Syrian armed forces leveled the downtown area when they crushed a local rising against the government.

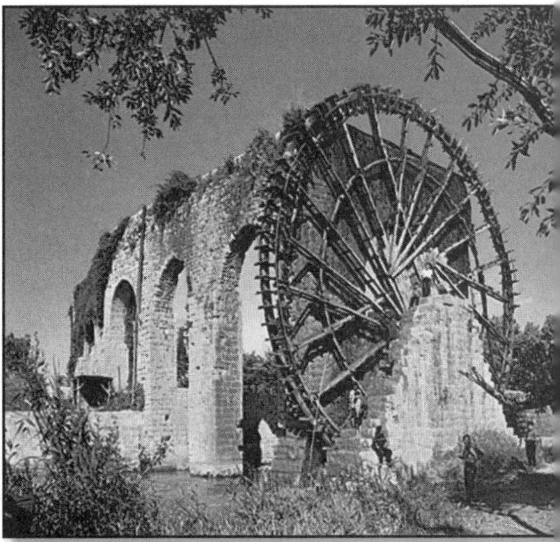

Waterwheel, Hamāh, Syria. Ray Manley/ Shostal Associates

DEMOGRAPHIC TRENDS

Syria's population is growing at a rate somewhat higher than the world average. The country's birth rate is higher than that of most neighbouring countries and is also higher than the world average. Life expectancy in Syria, while lower than in most neighbouring countries, is well above the world average. At the beginning of the 21st century, Syria's population was on the whole quite young, with almost two-fifths of Syrians younger than age 15 and some two-thirds younger than 30.

Only about half the country's land can support population, and about half the population is concentrated in the country's urban centres. The desert steppe, which has the country's lowest population density, is inhabited largely by Bedouins and oasis dwellers. Population density varies considerably in the rest of the country and is highest in the northwest and southwest and in the northeast. It is also fairly high along the banks of the major rivers.

Regional conflict has affected migration patterns in the country. Much of the population of the Golan Heights was expelled to other parts of Syria after Israel took control

Aleppo

Aleppo is the principal city of northern Syria and the country's largest city. It is situated in the northwestern part of the country, about 30 miles (50 km) south of the Turkish border. Aleppo is located at the crossroads of great commercial routes and lies some 60 miles (100 km) from both the Mediterranean Sea (west) and the Euphrates River (east).

The city's Arabic name, Ḥalab, is of ancient Semitic origin and is first mentioned in texts at the end of the 3rd millennium BCE. In the 18th century BCE Ḥalab was the capital of the Amorite kingdom of Yamkhad, and it subsequently came under Hittite, Egyptian, Mitannian, and again Hittite rule during the 17th to 14th centuries BCE. In succeeding centuries it achieved some independence as a Hittite principality. It was conquered by the Assyrians in the 8th century BCE, was controlled by the Achaemenian Persians from the 6th to the 4th century BCE, and then fell into the hands of the Seleucids, who rebuilt it and renamed it Beroea. It became a first-ranking city of the Hellenistic period and a great commercial entrepôt between the Mediterranean region and the lands farther east. The city was absorbed into the Roman province of Syria in the 1st century BCE. It prospered under Byzantine rule but was pillaged and burned by the Persian Sāsānian king Khosrow I in 540 CE. In 637 the city was conquered by the Arabs, under whom it reverted to its old name, Ḥalab.

In the 10th century CE the Ḥamdānid dynasty established itself in Aleppo as an independent principality, and the city had a brilliant cultural life under their rule. In the 12th century Aleppo became a centre of Muslim resistance to the Crusaders, who besieged it unsuccessfully in 1124–25. In 1260 Aleppo was taken by the Mongols, who massacred its inhabitants. After an interval of several centuries under the Mamlūks, the city was incorporated in 1516 into the Ottoman Empire, under which it underwent a remarkable commercial revival, becoming the principal market in the Levant. Its prosperity continued until the end of the 18th century, and full economic recovery came in 1880 with the arrival of the railroad. In the 20th century the city became an industrial centre rivaling Damascus, and by the 21st century it had surpassed the capital in size.

of the region in 1967. Many, along with their descendants, continue to be internally displaced. After the creation of Israel and the first of the Arab-Israeli wars, some 80,000 Palestinian Arabs found refuge in Syria, a population that is estimated to have since expanded to number more than 400,000. Likewise, with the outbreak of the Iraq War in 2003, Syria absorbed more than one million Iraqi refugees.

The process of socialist transformation under the Baʿth (Arabic: "Renaissance") Party and, less rigorously, under President Ḥafiz al-Assad caused much social, political, and economic turmoil and led to emigration among the wealthy and among some religious minorities. Increasing numbers of workers and professionals have been leaving the country since the 1950s for other Arab countries, the United States, and western Europe, movement that has caused an alarming drain on the Syrian workforce.

Golan Heights, near the Syrian-Israeli border. Keystone

CHAPTER 2

The Syrian Economy

Socialism became the official economic policy in 1963. Since then the trend has been toward socialist transformation and industrialization. In commerce, state control is mainly restricted to foreign-exchange operations. Small private businesses and cooperatives are still in operation, and the retail trade is still part of the private sector, in spite of competition from consumer cooperatives in the large cities. The government controls the most vital sectors of the country's economy and regulates private business. The state operates the oil refineries, the large electricity plants, the railways, and various manufacturing plants.

The government encourages private savings by paying higher rates of interest on deposits and by guaranteeing investment by citizens of other Arab countries. There are severe restrictions on all luxury imports. At the same time, strenuous efforts are made to mobilize economic potential, combat underemployment, and discourage emigration. In spite of modest steps toward privatization since 1990, the Syrian government has been largely hesitant to pursue economic liberalization, wary of its potential to endanger political stability.

AGRICULTURE, FORESTRY, AND FISHING

Agriculture constitutes an important source of income. It provides work for about one-sixth of the population, including a significant proportion of townspeople. Wheat is the most important food crop, although its production is constantly subject to great fluctuations in precipitation. Sugar beet production is also significant. Barley, corn (maize), and millet are the other important grains. Cotton is the largest and most reliable export crop. Lentils are a major domestic food, but they also are exported. Other fruits and vegetables include tomatoes, potatoes, melons, and onions. Olives, grapes, and apples are grown at high altitudes, while citrus fruits are cultivated along the coast. High-grade tobacco is grown in the area around Latakia. Raising livestock, including sheep, cattle, camels, and poultry, is also an important agricultural activity.

Forests make up a small percentage of the country's total area. Most of the country's timber has to be imported. Syria's small number of fishermen use small and medium-size boats. The annual fish catch includes sardines, tuna, groupers, tunny, and both red and gray mullet.

RESOURCES AND POWER

Syria's principal limestone quarries are located north and west of Damascus, especially near the city of Aleppo, which itself is built of limestone. Basalt, used for road pavement, is quarried in areas such as those near Ḥimṣ and Aleppo. Marl is used in the cement industry. The main quarries are in the vicinity of Damascus and Aleppo and at Al-Rastan. Phosphate ore is mined in areas near Tadmur, and rock salt is extracted from the mid-Euphrates region. Asphalt and gypsum are also mined, and table salt is produced from the salt lakes. Syria has scattered reserves of chrome and manganese.

Petroleum in commercial quantities was first discovered in the northeast in 1956. Among the most important oil fields are those of Suwaydiyyah, Qaratshūk, and Rumaylān, near Dayr al-Zawr. The fields are a natural extension of the Iraqi fields of Mosul and Kirkūk. Petroleum became Syria's leading natural resource and chief export after 1974. Production peaked in the mid-1990s, however, before beginning a steady decline. Natural gas was

Euphrates Dam

The Euphrates Dam, also called the Ṭabaqah (or Tabqa) Dam, is situated on the Euphrates River in north-central Syria. The dam, which is located 30 miles (50 km) upriver from the town of Al-Raqqah, was begun in 1968. Its construction prompted an intense archaeological excavation of the area around the town of Ṭabaqah. The dam is of earth-fill construction, some 197 feet (60 m) high and 2.8 miles (4.5 km) long. It was completed in 1973, and the reservoir behind the dam, Lake Al-Assad, began filling. The lake at its fullest extent is approximately 50 miles (80 km) long and averages 5 miles (8 km) in width. The accompanying power plant was inaugurated in 1978. Electrification subsequently reached to even the remotest villages in Al-Jazīrah (the area to the east of the Euphrates). Several irrigation schemes are associated with the project.

discovered at the field of Jbessa in 1940. Since that time natural gas production in Syria has expanded to form an important energy export. Additionally, some of the country's oil-fired power stations have been converted to run on natural gas, freeing more Syrian petroleum for export.

Raw phosphates were discovered in 1962. Some of the richest beds are located at Khunayfis, Ghadīr al-Jamal, and Wadi Al-Rakhim. Iron ore is found in the Zabadānī region. Asphalt has been found northeast of Latakia and west of Dayr al-Zawr.

Syria's primary source of power is derived from local oil supplies, and domestic natural gas reserves are becoming an increasingly important resource as well. Electricity is largely generated by thermal stations fired by natural gas or oil. With the exception of the Euphrates River, rivers flowing through Syria produce only small amounts of hydroelectric power. There are small hydroelectric stations, such as those on the Orontes and Baradā rivers, and a larger hydroelectric development at the Euphrates Dam at Ṭabaqah (inaugurated in 1978). However, insufficient dam maintenance, coupled with Turkish usage upstream and unpredictable precipitation, have decreased productivity.

Owing in part to the increasing industrialization initiatives of the late 20th century, Syria's electricity supply struggled to meet demand. In the early 21st century, several new thermal power stations were completed, largely alleviating shortages. In light of increasing demand, further expansion of the infrastructure continued to be needed, though Syria was able to export electricity to some of its neighbours, including Iraq and Lebanon.

MANUFACTURING

Wool, cotton, and nylon textiles are Syria's most important manufactures, and mills are mainly in Aleppo, Damascus, Ḥimṣ, and Ḥamāh. Natural silk is also produced. Also of importance are the technical engineering industries, most of which are located in Damascus. Chemical and industrial engineering products include cement; glass panes, bottles, and utensils; pharmaceuticals; plywood; and batteries.

The food-processing industry produces salt, vegetable oils, cotton cake, canned fruit and vegetables, tobacco, and a variety of dairy products. Other industries include the preparation of superphosphates and urea and petroleum refining.

Most of the traditional handmade manufactures—damask steel, swords and blades, brass and copper work, wood engravings, gold and silver ornaments, mother-of-pearl inlays, silk brocades—have decreased since the introduction of industrial processing.

FINANCE

The Central Bank of Syria issues the national currency, the Syrian pound, and exercises control over all other banks that operate in the country. The Commercial Bank of Syria finances trade, markets agricultural products, and carries out foreign-exchange operations. The Real Estate Bank finances the building industry and carries out all ordinary banking operations. An industrial development bank finances the private industrial sector, while an agricultural bank extends loans to farmers and agricultural cooperatives. The Popular Credit Bank makes loans to small manufacturers, artisans, and production cooperatives. There is a nationalized insurance company. Since 2000 a number of small private banks have been established as part of the gradual approach toward liberal economic reform. A stock exchange, the Damascus Securities Exchange, formally opened for trading in Damascus in 2009.

During the Cold War, Syria was offered financial and technical assistance free or at minimum interest rates from socialist countries such as China, Bulgaria, and the Soviet Union, and it has continued to receive aid at favourable conditions from China into the 21st century. At the end of the 20th century, Syria received substantial sums from Saudi Arabia and Kuwait for its support in the Persian Gulf War (1990–91). Aid with more stringent conditions has been sought from France and other Western countries.

TRADE

Syria has an unfavourable balance of trade, a deficit that is offset by revenues from tourism, transit trade returns, foreign aid, and earnings of Syrians overseas. Goods from Russia, China, and regional neighbours account for the bulk of Syria's imports. Major import items include refined petroleum, basic manufactures, foodstuffs, machinery and transport equipment, and chemicals. Italy, France, and Saudi Arabia consume a significant proportion of Syrian exports, which include petroleum, phosphates, ginned cotton, cottonseeds, barley, lentils, cotton and woolen fabrics, dried fruit, vegetables, skins, and raw wool. Foreign trade is regulated by the state.

Awe-inspiring ruins and other historical gems such as the Khan Assad Basha draw crowds of tourists into Syria, which is an excellent economic stimulus. Louai Beshara/AFP/Getty Images

SERVICES

Syria's service sector contributes heavily to the country's overall income, and at the beginning of the 21st century the sector employed a significant proportion of the country's workforce. Syria attracts tourism with a rich treasure trove of historical attractions that includes ancient and classical ruins, Muslim and Christian religious sites, and Crusader and medieval Islamic architecture. Some of these have been designated UNESCO World Heritage sites. Most tourists come from Arab countries, Iran, and Turkey, attracted to Syria's relatively mild summer climate and popular entertainment. A much smaller proportion of tourists come from Europe and the United States. Privatization of the tourism sector stimulated growth in revenues during the 1990s. Since the early 2000s, privatization in the areas of real estate, insurance, and trade has played a greater role in stimulating growth.

LABOUR AND TAXATION

The General Federation of Workers was founded in 1938 and has grown tremendously in power and scope. Composed only of industrial employees, it is represented on industrial boards and is responsible for a wide range of social services. There is also a federation for artisans and vocational workers, and there are associations for the professions and a General Federation of Farmers. Trade unions are obliged to organize under the Baʿth-controlled General Federation of Trade Unions.

Labour legislation establishes minimum-wage limits, prohibits child labour, and organizes relations between workers and employers. But economic and social conditions as well as the extent of unemployment, make rigorous enforcement impractical. Employees in heavy industry receive the highest industrial wages, textile workers the lowest. State employees have more job security. The major portion of the average salary is generally spent on housing and food.

Tax income accounts for more than one-third of governmental revenue. Indirect taxes, which produce the most tax revenue, are levied on industrial products, customs, exports, and state domains. Direct taxes are levied on wages, circulating capital, livestock, and the transfer of property.

TRANSPORTATION

Syria's road network is the chief means of transporting goods and passengers. Major roads include the highway between Damascus and Aleppo and the road between Damascus and Baghdad.

Syria's railways are well developed. A northern line runs northeastward from Aleppo into Turkey and then east along the border to Al-Qāmishlī, where it crosses the northeastern extremity of Syria en route to Baghdad. The Hejaz Railway links Damascus to Amman, and another runs from Aleppo to Tripoli. Aleppo and Damascus are also linked by rail. Smaller lines run between Ḥimṣ and Rīyāq (Lebanon) and between Beirut and Damascus. A railway also runs from Latakia to Aleppo, Al-Ḥasakah (passing by the Euphrates Dam), and Al-Qāmishlī. Another line extends northwest from Aleppo to the Turkish border at Maydān Ikbiz. From Ḥimṣ a line runs west to the port of Ṭarṭūs, and a line also runs east to the phosphate mines near Tadmur, opening up the desert interior to the Mediterranean.

The country's chief ports, Latakia and Ṭarṭūs, were built after independence. Port commerce was dampened by the closure of the Syrian border with Iraq in the early 1980s, although with the border's reopening in the late 1990s, shipments to Iraq as part of the United Nations (UN) oil for food program boosted the Syrian shipping industry.

Syria has international airports at Damascus and Aleppo, and several domestic airports are located throughout the country, including those at Al-Qāmishlī,

Hejaz Railway

The Hejaz Railway is a railroad between Damascus and Medina (now in Saudi Arabia) and was one of the principal railroads of the Ottoman Empire. Its main line was constructed in 1900–08 and traversed 820 miles (1,320 km) of difficult country, from Damascus southward to Darʿā and thence over Transjordan (modern Jordan) via Al-Zarqāʾ, Al-Qaṭrānah, and Maʿān into northwestern Arabia, and inland via Dhāt al-Ḥajj and Al-ʿUlā to Medina. The major branch line, 100 miles (160 km) long, from Darʿā to Haifa on the Mediterranean coast of Palestine, was completed in 1905.

When the Arabs of the Hejaz revolted against Turkish rule in 1916, the track between Maʿān and Medina was put out of operation by Arab raids, largely inspired by the British military strategist T. E. Lawrence (Lawrence of Arabia). After the war the operative sections of the track were taken over by the Syrian, Palestinian, and Transjordanian governments. The section of the railway running from Maʿān, Jordan, to Medina was heavily damaged and was abandoned after 1917.

In the late 20th century the northern portion of the Hejaz Railway (also called the Hejaz-Jordan Railway) between Amman, Jordan, and Damascus was in use and carried mostly freight. To the south, between Amman and Wadi Al-Abyaḍ, the rail line was only partly in operational condition and was not being used. From Wadi Al-Abyaḍ via Maʿān to Baṭn al-Ghūl the southern continuation of the Hejaz Railway was also in use, as was the newer rail line (owned by the Aqaba Railway Corporation) between Baṭn al-Ghūl and Al-ʿAqabah, which opened in 1975. Phosphates from the mines at Wadi al-Abyaḍ and nearby Al Ḥasā were transported by rail to the port of Al-ʿAqabah on the Red Sea.

Latakia, Dayr al-Zawr, and Tadmur. International services connect Syria with Arab, other Asian, and European countries. Domestic and international services are provided by Syrian Arab Airlines.

CHAPTER 3

Syrian Government and Society

The constitution of 1973 declares that Syria constitutes an integral part of the Arab homeland, that all legislative power lies with the people, and that freedom of expression and equality before the law are guaranteed. However, the enforcement of these principles has been deficient. Especially from the late 1970s, constitutionally guaranteed rights were increasingly suppressed under President Ḥafiz al-Assad's rule.

Syria is a unitary multiparty republic with one legislative house. The regional (Syrian) leadership of the Ba‘th Party elects the head of state, who must be a Muslim, and appoints the cabinet, which exercises legislative as well as executive powers. Legislative power is vested in the People's Council, members of which are elected by popular vote to four-year terms. The Ba‘th Party is constitutionally guaranteed an absolute majority.

Local Government

Syria is divided into governorates (one of which, Damascus, is a governorate-level city), *manāṭiq* (districts), and *nawāḥī* (subdistricts). The governors, or *muḥāfiẓūn*, enjoy some power within their administrative divisions, but their centralized local government depends upon the minister of the interior in the national government.

Justice

The principles of Syrian law and equity derive basically from Islamic jurisprudence and secondarily from the French civil code. Summary courts try civil, commercial, and penal cases. The headquarters of each administrative district has a First Instance Court for criminal cases. The capital city of each governorate also has a court of appeal.

Damascus houses a high court of appeal and a constitutional court, as well as a military tribunal and the mufti's court for the maintenance of Islamic law. Various non-Muslim sects each have their own courts with jurisdiction over personal-status cases.

POLITICAL PROCESS

Most authority is wielded by the ruling Ba'th Party. Since its foundation in the 1940s, the party has undergone radical internal changes as a result of successive coups d'état and internal power struggles. The party has branch organizations in many Arab countries, each headed by its own regional leadership. The organs of administration are the National Command, the Regional Command, and the People's Council; the latter operates as a legislature. The supreme national leadership is composed of representatives from each regional branch, who are elected by their own party congresses. The regional leadership for Syria is the highest authority in the country but is subordinate to the national leadership. Actual power resides in the presidency. All political parties are officially linked together as the National Progressive Front, which is dominated by the Ba'th Party.

Although Syria has universal adult suffrage, elections are generally not held by international observers as free and fair. Women are able to participate in the political system and have held a number of positions, and in the early 21st century almost one-eighth of the members of parliament were women. The 'Alawite religious minority has dominated Syrian politics since the 1960s.

SECURITY

Military service is compulsory for all adult males, and college students receive deferments. Military service

Ba'th Party

The Ba'th Party (in full, Arab Socialist Ba'th Party, or Arab Socialist Renaissance Party; Arabic: Ḥizb al-Ba'th al-'Arabī al-Ishtirākī) is an Arab political party advocating the formation of a single Arab socialist nation. It has branches in many Middle Eastern countries and was the ruling party in Syria from 1963 and in Iraq from 1968 to 2003.

The Ba'th Party was founded in 1943 in Damascus by Michel 'Aflaq and Ṣalāḥ al-Dīn al-Bīṭār, adopted its constitution in 1947, and in 1953 merged with the Syrian Socialist Party to form the Arab Socialist Ba'th (Renaissance) Party. The Ba'th Party espoused nonalignment and opposition to imperialism and colonialism, took inspiration from what it considered the positive values of Islam, and attempted to ignore or transcend class divisions. Its structure was highly centralized and authoritarian.

The Syrian Ba'thists took power in 1963, but factionalism between "progressives" and "nationalists" was severe until 1970, when Ḥafiz al-Assad of the "nationalists" secured control. In Iraq the Ba'thists took power briefly in 1963 and regained it in 1968, after which the party's power became concentrated under Iraqi leader Ṣaddām Ḥussein. Differences between the Iraqi and Syrian wings of the Ba'th Party precluded unification of the two countries. Within both countries the Ba'thists formed fronts with smaller parties, including at times the communists. In Syria the main internal threat to Ba'th hegemony stemmed from the Muslim Brotherhood, while in Iraq Kurdish and Shī'ite opposition was endemic. The Iraqi branch of the party was toppled in 2003 as a result of the Iraq War.

provides general and technical—as well as military—education and training. The army is the largest contingent of Syria's armed forces and is responsible for defense, public works, road construction, and public health. There is also an air force, a small navy, and reserve units for all three branches. Palestinian Arab guerrilla organizations operate from Syria and have training facilities there.

HEALTH AND WELFARE

Most endemic diseases in Syria have been eliminated. Health facilities include state and private hospitals and sanatoriums, as well as hospitals and outpatient clinics of the armed forces. There are also a number of public and private outpatient clinics, as well as maternal and child care, antituberculosis, malaria eradication, and rural health centres. Child mortality is caused mostly by measles and diseases of the digestive and respiratory systems. Tuberculosis and trachoma are widespread, particularly among the Bedouin, peasants, and residents of poorer urban areas.

Health conditions and sanitation in the cities, towns, and larger villages are generally satisfactory. Running water is supplied to almost all houses, buildings, and public places. Each municipality maintains its streets and regularly collects refuse. Although the government has offered incentives for doctors to serve rural areas, medical services are unevenly distributed, with most doctors concentrated in the large cities.

The Ministry of Social Welfare and Labour is empowered to find work for, and distribute cash allowances to, the unemployed. The ministry also encourages such youth activities as athletics, scouting, literacy campaigns, and the organization of cooperatives. The government gives substantial grants to private welfare societies.

The high birth rate in Syria has caused family lands to be broken up into ever smaller lots and has reduced the standard of living of many rural inhabitants.

HOUSING

The old houses in Damascus are built of soft unbaked bricks, wood, and stone. Contemporary buildings are built of concrete, while hewn stone is reserved for official buildings, mosques, and churches.

The pace of change from an agricultural to an industrial economy, and the accompanying migration to the cities, led to an acute shortage of housing. Aggravating the shortage, young adult males migrating from rural areas to the cities are increasingly breaking with tradition by leaving their parental homes for their own. The Ministry of Municipal and Rural Affairs undertakes the construction of blocks of low-income flats in the cities.

EDUCATION

About four-fifths of the Syrian population is literate, although literacy rates are significantly higher among men than among women. Schooling, which begins at age six, is divided into six years of compulsory primary, three years of lower secondary, and three years of upper secondary education. Lower and upper secondary schools provide general (which prepares for university entrance) or vocational curricula. Secondary schools are open to all elementary students who wish to continue their education. Within this framework, increased attention is being given to technical education. The University of Damascus, founded in 1923, is the country's oldest university. Other universities include the University of Aleppo (1960), Tishrīn University (1971) in Latakia, and Al-Ba'th University (1979) in Ḥimṣ. All levels of education have been expanded substantially since 1963.

CHAPTER 4

SYRIAN CULTURAL LIFE

Contemporary Syrian culture blends Arab, Mediterranean, and European elements. Syrians are keenly interested in international politics and culture, which many follow through national radio and television programs as well as those broadcast from other Middle Eastern countries and from Europe. The Ministry of Culture and National Guidance has been active in directing and promoting the nation's cultural life. An important objective has been the affirmation of the Arab national character in the face of foreign cultural influences.

DAILY LIFE AND SOCIAL CUSTOMS

The family is the heart of Syrian social life. Frequent visits and exchanges of invitations for meals among family members are integral to daily living. Although formally arranged marriages are becoming less frequent, parents ordinarily wield decisive authority in approving or rejecting a match. Marriage to members of one's religion is the norm. Muslim men may marry non-Muslim women, although the reverse is prohibited. Interdenominational marriages among Christians are legal but require permission from both denominations. Neighbourly relations and friendships among members of different religions are common in Syrian cities.

A visible expression of Syria's cultural eclecticism is demonstrated in its range of clothing styles. While some women choose the latest European fashions, others are completely veiled. Older men in traditional black baggy trousers contrast with youths sporting Western styles.

Syrian Muslims observe the major religious holidays of Ramadan, ʿĪd al-Fiṭr ("Festival of Breaking Fast," marking the end of Ramadan) and ʿĪd al-Aḍḥā ("Festival of the Sacrifice," marking the culmination of the annual pilgrimage to Mecca). Syrian Christians freely celebrate the holidays of the Christian tradition, including Christmas and Easter.

Syrian cuisine makes use of a wide range of ingredients and styles of preparation. Lemon, garlic, onions, and spices are often featured prominently, for example. *Kibbeh*—ball-shaped or flat diamond-cut bulgur (cracked wheat) shells filled with ground beef or lamb, spices, and pine nuts—are enjoyed, oftentimes served with yogurt. Grapevine leaves are stuffed with spiced mixtures of lamb or beef and rice and simmered with lemon juice; variants also exist using cabbage leaves and a lemon-tomato broth. Meat pies and spinach pies are also enjoyed, and fruits, vegetables, and grains are staples in Syrian dishes. Flat bread, cheeses, salads, and olives are often a fixture of the *mazzah* (mezes), a spread of smaller dishes served together. Syrian pastries, some of which require substantial skill to prepare, are of a wide variety.

Syrian cuisine features a variety of spices, making for a varied menu. Richard Ross/The Image Bank/Getty Images

THE ARTS

The artistic representation of animal or human life is proscribed by Islam, and until World War I public figurative art in Syria was restricted to geometric, vegetative, and animal designs as manifest in the arts of arabesque and calligraphy, which adorn most palaces and mosques. Following World War I, drawing was taught in the schools, and talented artists began to emerge. Sculpture is mainly confined to decorations hewn in white marble. Damascus is particularly famous for this type of sculpture, and beautiful examples of it can be seen in its palaces and public buildings.

Poet 'Alī Aḥmad Sa'īd is better known as Adonis to the increasing numbers of literary-minded Syrians. John MacDougall/AFP/Getty Images

Short-story writing and poetry have flourished, as in the widely read works of Nizār Qabbānī and 'Alī Aḥmad Sa'īd ("Adonis"). The country's leading playwright, Sa'dallah Wannus (1941–97) has an international reputation for his politically forthright productions. The National Theatre and other theatrical and folk-dance

Nizār Qabbānī

(b. March 21, 1923, Damascus, Syria—d. April 30, 1998, London, England)

Nizār Qabbānī was a Syrian diplomat and poet whose subject matter, at first strictly erotic and romantic, grew to embrace political issues as well. Written in simple but eloquent language, his verses, some of which were set to music, won the hearts of countless Arabic speakers throughout the Middle East and Africa.

Qabbānī, who was born into a middle-class merchant family, was also the grandnephew of the pioneering Arab playwright Abū Khalīl Qabbānī. He studied law at the University of Damascus (LL.B., 1945), then began his varied career as a diplomat. He served in the Syrian embassies in Egypt, Turkey, Lebanon, Britain, China, and Spain before retiring in 1966 and moving to Beirut, where he founded the Manshurāt Nizār Qabbānī, a publishing company. Meanwhile, he also wrote much poetry, at first in classic forms, then in free verse, which he helped establish in modern Arabic poetry. His poetic language is noted for capturing the rhythms of everyday Syrian speech.

The suicide of his sister, who was unwilling to marry a man she did not love, had a profound effect on Qabbānī, and much of his poetry concerns the experiences of women in traditional Muslim society. Verses on the beauty and desirability of women filled Qabbānī's first four collections. In *Qaṣā'id min Nizār Qabbānī* (1956; "Poems by Nizār Qabbānī"), a turning point in his art, he expressed resentment of male chauvinism. It also included his famed "Bread, Hashish and Moon," a harsh attack on weak, impoverished Arab societies that live in a haze of drug-induced fantasies. Thereafter, he often wrote from a woman's viewpoint and advocated social freedoms for women. His *Hawāmish 'alā daftar al-naksah* (1967; "Marginal Notes on the Book of Defeat") was a stinging critique of unrealistic Arab leadership during the June 1967 war with Israel. Among his more than 20 poetry collections, the most noted volumes are *Ḥabībatī* (1961; "My Beloved") and *Al-rasm bi-al-kalimāt* (1966; "Drawing with Words"). *Qaṣā'id Ḥubb 'Arabiyyah* ("Arabian Love Poems") was published in 1993.

companies give regular performances. In the realm of popular television, theatre, and cinema, Durayd Lahham's comic figure Ghawwar, a sort of "wise fool," enjoys a popular following throughout the Arab world. Syrians produce and listen to styles of popular music shared by much of the Arab world. Renowned Syrian musical artists include singer and *'ūd* player Farid al-Atrash and his sister Amal, known as Asmahan, who was a popular singer and actor.

CULTURAL INSTITUTIONS

National folk traditions have been emphasized by the state, which has established a museum for national folk traditions in Damascus. The capital also contains the National Museum and separate museums for agriculture and military history. Archaeological museums are located in Aleppo and at major sites. Of numerous libraries throughout Syria, Al-Assad National Library, al-Ẓāhiriyyah, and the library associated with the University of Damascus are among the country's most important.

The Ministry of Culture has established an Arab institute of music and has made available a plethora of courses in the figurative and applied arts, as well as centres for teaching the domestic arts. The Arabic Language Academy in Damascus, founded in 1919, is the oldest such academy in the Arab world.

A number of Syria's archaeological and historic features have been recognized by UNESCO as World Heritage sites. These include the ancient cities of Damascus, Aleppo, and Bostra, the site of Palmyra, and the Crusader-period fortresses of Krak des Chevaliers ("Castle of the Knights") and Qal'at Salāḥ al-Din ("Fortress of Saladin").

Krak des Chevaliers

Krak des Chevaliers (French-Arabic: "Castle of the Knights") is the greatest fortress built by European Crusaders in Syria and Palestine, one of the most notable surviving examples of medieval military architecture. Built in western Syria near the northern border of present-day Lebanon, it occupied the site of an earlier Muslim stronghold. It was built by the Knights of St. John (Hospitallers), who held it from 1142 till 1271, when it was captured by the Mamlūk sultan Baybars I. It has two concentric towered walls separated by a wide moat and could accommodate a garrison of 2,000 men. In 2006 the fortress (along with the Qalʿat Salāḥ al-Dīn ["Fortress of Saladin"]) was designated a UNESCO World Heritage site.

SPORTS AND RECREATION

Football (soccer) is the country's most popular sport, and Syrians closely follow both Arab and European matches broadcast on national television. Weight lifting, judo, and karate are popular in the cities, and health clubs and gyms are becoming increasingly common in the capital. There are stadiums in Damascus, Aleppo, and Latakia, where occasional sporting events are held. The government-run Institute for Sports Education is in charge of organizing these sporting events, and the General Union of Sports, which is also funded by the government, promotes sports in rural areas to underprivileged children. Syria first competed in the 1948 Games in London and later won its first medal in men's heavyweight freestyle wrestling at the 1984 Olympic Games.

Leisure activities are by no means limited to sporting events. Many Syrians enjoy frequent family outings to favourite picnic spots by streams or to mountain resorts.

MEDIA AND PUBLISHING

The majority of Syria's publishing industry is concentrated in Damascus. Magazines and journals are run mostly by official or semiofficial bodies. Daily, weekly, and fortnightly newspapers are published, and all newspapers are subject to government restrictions. Leading dailies include *Tishrīn*, *Al-Ba'th*, and the government publication *Al-Thawrah*. The Syrian Arab News Agency (SANA) is the country's official, state-run news bureau.

Radio and television broadcasting in Syria is overseen by the Directorate-General of Radio and Television. Syrian radio broadcasting began in 1945 and grew to become a powerful rival of the local press. Radio broadcasts are mainly in Arabic but also in English, French, Turkish, Russian, Hebrew, and German, and they reach almost every Syrian home. The country's first private radio station, Al-Madina FM, was launched in 2005.

The Syrian Television Service, which was established in 1960, reaches a large audience throughout the country. Television broadcasting includes educational and cultural programs, drama, music, news, and sports. Syrian television series are becoming increasingly popular throughout the Arab world. Government control once shaped and limited the public's perception of current events, but, as satellite dishes became more common, Syrians gained access to a broader selection of Middle Eastern and European programming.

CHAPTER 5

Syria: Past and Present

The earliest prehistoric remains of human habitation found in Syria and Palestine (stone implements, with bones of elephants and horses) are of the Middle Paleolithic Period. In the next stage are remains of rhinoceroses and of men who are classified as intermediate between Neanderthal and modern types. The Mesolithic Period is best represented by the Natufian culture, which is spread along, and some distance behind, the coast of the Levant. The Natufians supported life by fishing, hunting, and gathering the grains that, in their wild state, were indigenous to the country. This condition was gradually superseded by the domestication of animals, the cultivation of crops, and the production of pottery. Excavations at Mureybet in Syria have revealed a settlement where the inhabitants made pottery and cultivated einkorn, a single-grained wheat, as early as the 9th millennium BCE. Metallurgy, particularly the production of bronze (an alloy of copper and tin), appeared after the mid-4th millennium BCE. The first cities emerged shortly thereafter.

From Early History to the Hellenistic and Roman Periods

History begins with the invention of writing, which took place in southern Babylonia perhaps about 3000 BCE, the script being an original picture character that developed later into cuneiform. Modern research, however, suggests that clay tokens found at numerous ancient Middle Eastern sites from as early as 8000 BCE may have been used as an archaic recording system and ultimately led to the invention of writing.

By the mid-3rd millennium BCE, various Semitic peoples had migrated into Syria-Palestine and Babylonia. Knowledge of this period has been enormously enhanced by the excavations at Tall Mardīkh (ancient Ebla), south of Aleppo. The palace has yielded more than 17,000 inscribed clay tablets, dated to about 2600–2500 BCE, which detail the social, religious, economic, and political life of this thriving and powerful Syrian kingdom. The language of Ebla has been identified as Northwest Semitic.

About 2320 BCE Lugalzaggisi, the Sumerian ruler of Erech (Uruk), boasted of an empire that stretched to the Mediterranean. It was short-lived. He was defeated by the Semite Sargon of Akkad, who became the greatest conqueror and most famous name in Babylonian history. Sargon led his armies up the Euphrates to the "cedar mountain" (the Amanus) and beyond. Ebla was destroyed either by Sargon at this time or perhaps by his grandson, Naram-sin (*c.* 2275 BCE), and the region of Syria became part of the Akkadian Empire. But the dynasty of Akkad was soon overthrown as its centre and superseded by the dynasties first of Guti and then of Ur.

Nothing certain is known about the authority (if any) that the kings of Ur exercised in Syria, so far away from their capital. The end of their dynasty, however, was brought about chiefly by the pressure of a new Semitic migration from Syria, this time of the Amorites (i.e., the Westerners), as they were called in Babylonia. Between about 2000 and 1800 BCE they covered both Syria and Mesopotamia with a multitude of small principalities and cities, mostly governed by rulers bearing some name characteristic of the Semitic dialect that the Amorites spoke. The period of Amorite ascendancy is vividly mirrored in the Mari Letters, a great archive of royal correspondence found at the site of Mari, near the modern frontier with Iraq. Among the principal figures mentioned are the celebrated lawgiver Hammurabi of Babylon (himself an Amorite) and a king of Aleppo, part of whose kingdom was the city of Alalakh, on the Orontes near what was later Antioch. Around 1600 BCE northern Syria, including the cities of Alalakh, Aleppo, and Ebla in its Amorite phase, suffered destruction at the hands of the aggressive Hittite kings, Hattusilis I or Mursilis I, from central Anatolia.

Earlier, in the 18th century BCE, a movement of people from Syria had begun in the opposite direction. This resulted in the Hyksos infiltration and eventual seizure (*c.* 1674 BCE) of regal authority in northern Egypt, which was subject to this foreign domination for 108 years. The mixed multitude of the Hyksos certainly included Hurrians, who, not being Aryans themselves, were under the rule and influence of Aryans and learned from them the use of light chariots and horses in warfare, which they introduced into Egypt, Syria, and Mesopotamia. The Hurrians established the kingdom of Mitanni, with its centre east of the Euphrates, and this was for long the dominant power in Syria, reaching its height in the 15th century BCE. Documentary evidence for the Mitanni period comes from excavations made in the 1970s at Tall Hadidi (ancient Azu), at the edge of Lake Al-Assad.

But other nations were growing at the same time, and in the 14th century Syria was the arena in which at least four great competitors contended. The Hurrians were first in possession, and they maintained friendly relations with Egypt, which, after expelling the Hyksos, had established a vast sphere of influence in Palestine and Syria under the kings of the 18th dynasty. Third of the powers disputing Syria in the 14th century were the Hittites, who finally, under their greatest warrior, Suppiluliumas (*c.* 1350 BCE), not only defeated the kingdom of Mitanni but established a firm dominion of their own in northern Syria with its principal centres at Aleppo and Carchemish. Fourth was the rising kingdom of Assyria, which became a serious contender in the reign of Ashur-uballit I.

This was the period of the Amarna Letters, which vividly illustrate the decline of Egyptian influence in Syria (especially under Akhenaton), the distress or duplicity of local governors, and the rivalry of the aforesaid powers. Egyptians and Hittites continued their struggle into the 13th century until finally the Battle of Kadesh (*c.* 1290 BCE) led to a treaty maintaining equal balance. Assyria had already swept away the remains of Mitanni but itself soon fell into decline, and the Hittites were not long afterward driven from their centre in Asia Minor by the migration of "peoples of the sea," Western invaders from the isles of the Aegean and from Europe. The dislocation of peoples at this time apparently also led to the migration into northern Syria of a related Indo-European group from Anatolia, the so-called Neo-Hittites. They established a number of principalities, and the area became known as Hatti-land.

As early as the 14th century various documents mention the Akhlame, who were forerunners of another vast movement of Semitic tribes called, generically, Aramaeans. By the end of the 13th century these had covered with their small and loose principalities the whole of central and northern Syria. The Assyrians were able to guard their homeland from this penetration, however, and henceforth much of the warfare of Assyrian kings was aimed at the Aramaean states of Syria. At about the same time as the Aramaean invasion, the exodus of Israelite tribes from Egypt was proceeding. Toward the end of the 11th century, as the Israelites established a kingdom centred upon Jerusalem, the Aramaeans set up their principal kingdom at Damascus. The wars between kings of

Judah or of Israel and kings of Aram make up much of Old Testament history.

But the most formidable enemies of the Aramaeans and often the Hebrews were the great military kings of the Assyrians. In the 9th and 8th centuries BCE the Assyrian Empire was established over the west. At the Battle of Karkar in 853 BCE, Shalmaneser III of Assyria was opposed by Bar-Hadad I (Hebrew: Ben-hadad I; throne name Hadadezer; Akkadian: Adad-idri) of Damascus, Ahab of Israel, and 12 vassal monarchs. In 732 BCE Damascus, the Syrian capital, was at length captured by Tiglath-pileser III. But campaigns against the Aramaeans and Neo-Hittites of northern Syria had to be undertaken by the Assyrians until almost the end of the Assyrian Empire. Culturally, the most important achievement of the Aramaeans was the bringing of the alphabet into general use for public and private business.

Before the close of the 8th century BCE, a massive southward movement of people, partly of Aryan descent, began from the north and west. Pressure of this movement upon the Assyrian dominions and homeland became ever more severe, and it deeply affected Syria also. In the 7th century there came the invasion of the Cimmerians, followed by the Scythians. To these and to the Medes, Assyria finally succumbed with the fall of Nineveh in 612 BCE. Nebuchadnezzar II, crown prince of Babylon, finally defeated the attempted rescue of Assyria by Necho II, king of Egypt, and annihilated his army at Carchemish in 605 BCE. In 597 BCE he captured Jerusalem and carried its people into exile. Thereafter, Syria was for half a century under the rule of Nebuchadnezzar's successors on the throne of Babylon.

But another and greater power, the Persians, then came to the fore. Under the leadership of Cyrus II they

Ebla

Ebla (modern Tall Mardīkh, also spelled Tell Mardikh) is an ancient city 33 miles (53 km) southwest of Aleppo in northwestern Syria. During the height of its power (*c.* 2600–2240 BCE), Ebla dominated northern Syria, Lebanon, and parts of northern Mesopotamia (modern Iraq) and enjoyed trade and diplomatic relations with states as far away as Egypt, Iran, and Sumer.

Part of Ebla's prosperity stemmed from its agricultural hinterland, in the rich plain of northern Syria, where barley, wheat, olives, figs, grapes, pomegranates, and flax were grown and cattle, sheep, goats, and pigs were raised. Beyond, Ebla controlled a group of 17 city-states, probably in what is now Lebanon and southeastern Turkey, areas rich in silver and timber. The city proper was a manufacturing and distribution centre. Linen and wool, including damask cloth, were the main products. Metalworking, including the smelting and alloying of gold, silver, copper, tin, and lead, was the second most important activity. Woodworking and the production of olive oil, wine, and beer also were important.

Trade was the third support of Ebla's economy. Cloth, manufactured goods, and olive oil were its main exports; imports included gold, silver, copper, tin, precious stones, and sheep. Because of its geographic location, Ebla grew wealthy on transit trade. Materials from Iran, Anatolia, and Cyprus were transshipped to states as distant as Sumer and Egypt. The Egyptian trade passed through Byblos.

Diplomacy and limited warfare supported Ebla's commercial activities. Emar, a city strategically located at the confluence of the Euphrates and Galikh rivers, was tied to Ebla by dynastic marriage. Khammazi was Ebla's commercial and diplomatic ally in Iran. Commercial treaties were drawn up with other cities. Mari, on the Euphrates River to the southeast, was Ebla's great commercial rival. Twice, an Eblaite army marched against it, and for a time Ebla ruled Mari through a military governor.

Nonhereditary kings governed Ebla for limited terms, and a council of elders shared in decision making. The manufacture of cloth was under the queen's charge. Fourteen governors appointed by the king ruled Ebla's departments, two of them in the city proper.

The religion of Ebla was polytheistic and primarily Canaanite. Dabir was the city's patron god, but Dagon, Sipish, Hadad, Balatu, and Astarte were also worshiped. The language of Ebla was a hitherto unknown Canaanite dialect, most closely akin to the Northwest Semitic languages. The script of the tablets, however, is Sumerian cuneiform, with closest similarity to tablets from Adab and Abū Salābīkh (now in Iraq). Texts reveal that Sumerian teachers came to Ebla, and the presence of a "Canal of Ebla" near Adab attests that Eblaites went to Sumer as well. Vocabularies, syllabaries, gazetteers, and student exercises that have been recovered show that Ebla was a major educational centre. The completeness of Ebla's texts, which at points duplicate fragmentary texts from Sumer, greatly enhances the modern study of Sumerian.

extended their conquests into Asia Minor and then came to a final collision with Babylon, which Cyrus occupied in 539 BCE. He sent back the exiled Jewish community to Jerusalem, encouraging them to rebuild their temple. In Darius I's great organization of the Persian dominions, Syria, with Palestine and Cyprus, was the fifth satrapy, bearing the name of "Across the River" (i.e., the Euphrates), with tribute fixed at 350 talents of silver. Damascus and the Phoenician cities were still the chief centres of Syria under the Persians, and in Sidon was the core of the Phoenician revolt against Artaxerxes III, which ended with the destruction of that city in 345 BCE. But by this time, the end of the Persian domination was at hand, and the Macedonians under Alexander the Great were about to bring the whole Middle East under Greek rule and influence.

Alexander invaded Asia Minor in 334 BCE, and his victory over the Persians at Issus in 333 was followed by the capture and enslavement of Tyre and Gaza. With the

Battle of Gaugamela and the destruction of Persepolis, the downfall of Persia was complete.

The Hellenistic Age

After Alexander's death in 323 BCE his marshals contended for control of the country until, after the Battle of Ipsus (301), Seleucus I Nicator gained the northern part and Ptolemy I Soter gained the southern (Coele Syria). This partition between the Seleucids and the Ptolemies was maintained for 100 years. Their administrative methods varied. In the south the Ptolemies respected the existing autonomous cities, imposed a bureaucratic system on the rest of the country, and established no colonies. The Seleucids divided the north into four satrapies and founded many cities and military colonies—among them Antioch, Seleucia Pieria, Apamea, and Laodicea—drawing on European settlers. Republics replaced kings in the Phoenician coastal cities of Tyre (274 BCE), Sidon, Byblos, and Aradus. Further political and cultural changes followed.

In 200 BCE (or perhaps as late as 198) Antiochus III (the Great) defeated Ptolemy V Epiphanes at Panium and secured control of southern Syria, where he introduced the satrapal system. His subsequent defeat by the Romans at Magnesia (December 190 or January 189 BCE), however, resulted in the loss of both his territory in Asia Minor and his prestige, thereby fundamentally weakening the Seleucid Empire, which ceased to be a Mediterranean power. Antiochus IV Epiphanes (ruled 175–163/4 BCE) stimulated the spread of Greek culture and political ideas in Syria by a policy of urbanization. Increased city organization and municipal autonomy involved greater decentralization of his kingdom. His attempted Hellenization of the Jews is well known.

Under the Seleucid kings, with rival claimants to the throne and constant civil war, Syria disintegrated. In the north the Seleucids controlled little more than the areas of Antioch and Damascus. Southern Syria was partitioned by three tribal dynasties: the Ituraeans, the Jews, and the Nabateans. The country was seized later by Tigranes II the Great of Armenia (83 BCE). He ruled until his defeat by Pompey, who ended years of anarchy by making Syria a Roman province (64–63 BCE).

Roman Provincial Organization

Pompey in the main accepted the status quo, but he reestablished a number of cities and reduced the kingdom of Judaea. Ten cities of the interior formed a league, the Decapolis. The native client kingdoms of Commagene, Ituraea, Judaea, and Nabataea were henceforth subjected to Roman Syria. Parthian invasions were thrown back in 51–50 and 40–39 BCE, and Mark Antony's extensive territorial gifts to Cleopatra (including Ituraea, Damascus, and Coele Syria) involved only temporary adjustments.

Under the early empire, Syria, which stretched northeast to the upper Euphrates and, until 73 CE, included eastern Cilicia, became one of the most important provinces. Its governor, a consular legate, generally commanded four legions until 70 CE. Administrative changes followed, as Rome gradually annexed the client kingdoms. Ituraea was incorporated (i.e., its territories were assigned to neighbouring cities) partly in 24 BCE, partly about 93 CE. Judaea became a separate province in 6 CE, governed by procurators (apart from the short-lived control by Herod Agrippa I, 41–44 CE), until the destruction of Jerusalem in 70. Then the governor was a praetorian legate in command of a legion. Next, under Hadrian, he was a consular with two legions, and the province was named Syria Palaestina.

Triumphal arch of Septimius Severus, Latakia, Syria. Sam Abboud/FPG

Commagene was annexed permanently by Vespasian in 72. The caravan city of Palmyra came under Roman control, possibly during Tiberius's reign. Finally, Nabataea was made the province of Arabia in 105, governed by a praetorian legate with one legion.

Syria itself was later divided by Septimius Severus into two provinces—Syria Coele in the north with two legions and Syria Phoenice with one. By the beginning of the 5th century it was subdivided into at least five provinces. The frontiers of Syria were guarded by a fortified limes system, which was thoroughly reorganized by Diocletian and his successors (particularly against cavalry attacks) and which endured until the Arab conquest. Much knowledge of this system of "defense in depth" has been obtained with the aid of aerial photography.

Economy and Culture

Syria's economic prosperity depended on its natural products (including wine, olives, vegetables, fruits, and nuts); industries (including purple dyeing, glassmaking at Sidon, linen and wool weaving, and metalwork); and control and organization of trade passing by caravan from the east to the Mediterranean through such centres as Palmyra, Damascus, Bostra, and Petra. Syria remained essentially rural. The urban upper and middle classes might be Hellenized, but the lower classes still spoke Aramaic and other Semitic dialects. Roman influences were naturally weaker than Greek, though the army at first helped the spread of Romanization.

The splendour of Syrian culture is seen in the magnificence of the cities. For example, ranking among the greatest cities of the empire, Antioch was the residence of the governor and later of the *comes Orientis*, who governed the diocese of the East. This brilliance is also evident in their schools of rhetoric, law, and medicine; in their art; in their literature and philosophy; and in the variety of their religions, both pagan and Christian.

Byzantine Syria

During the three centuries Syria was administered from Constantinople, its cultural and economic life remained active. Government became more bureaucratic, but it was efficient. In the 4th century, during the campaigns of Constantine I and Julian against Persia, Syria had again become a base of operations and at times endured Persian invasion. The Persian threat subsided during the 5th century, but it blazed up again in the 6th, when Arabs also added to the danger. The Persian Khosrow I captured Antioch itself (540); and in 573 the Persians were back again. The invasion of Khosrow II, which began in 606, was later rolled back by the victories of Heraclius, but the peace of 628 brought no tranquillity to Syria.

MEDIEVAL PERIOD

In the first half of the 7th century, Syria was absorbed into the expanding Islamic world. Arab Muslim forces had appeared on the southern border even before the death of the Prophet Muhammad in 632, but the real invasion took place in 633–634, with Khālid ibn al-Walīd as its most important leader. In 635 Damascus surrendered, its inhabitants being promised security for their lives, property, and churches, on payment of a poll tax. A counterattack by the emperor Heraclius was defeated at the Battle of the Yarmūk River in 636; by 640 the conquest was virtually complete.

Early Islamic Rule

The new rulers divided Syria into four districts (*junds*): Damascus, Ḥimṣ, Jordan, and Palestine (to which a fifth, Qinnasrīn, was later added). The Arab garrisons were kept apart in camps, and life went on much as before. Conversion to Islam had scarcely begun, apart from Arab tribes already settled in Syria. Except for the tribe of Ghassān, these all became Muslim. Christians and Jews were treated with

Khālid ibn al-Walīd

(d. 642)

Khālid ibn al-Walīd (byname: Sayf Allāh [Arabic: "Sword of God"]) was one of the two generals (with 'Amr ibn al-'Āṣ) of the enormously successful Islamic expansion under the Prophet Muhammad and his immediate successors, Abū Bakr and 'Umar.

Although he fought against Muhammad at Uḥud (625), Khālid was later converted and joined Muhammad in the conquest of Mecca in 629. Thereafter he commanded a number of conquests and missions in the Arabian Peninsula. After the death of Muhammad, Khālid recaptured a number of provinces that were breaking away from Islam. He was sent northeastward by the caliph Abū Bakr to invade Iraq, where he conquered Al-Ḥīrah. Crossing the desert, he aided in the conquest of Syria. And although the new caliph, 'Umar, formally relieved him of high command (for unknown reasons), Khālid remained the effective leader of the forces facing the Byzantine armies in Syria and Palestine.

Routing the Byzantine armies, he surrounded Damascus, which surrendered on Sept. 4, 635, and pushed northward. Early in 636 he withdrew south of the Yarmūk River before a powerful Byzantine force that advanced from the north and from the coast of Palestine. The Byzantine armies were composed mainly of Christian Arab, Armenian, and other auxiliaries, however. When many of these deserted the Byzantines, Khālid, reinforced from Medina and possibly from the Syrian Arab tribes, attacked and destroyed the remaining Byzantine forces along the ravines of the Yarmūk valley (Aug. 20, 636). Almost 50,000 Byzantine troops were slaughtered, which opened the way for many other Islamic conquests.

tolerance, and Nestorian and Jacobite Christians had better treatment than they had under Byzantium. The Byzantine form of administration remained, but the new Muslim tax system was introduced. From 639 the governor of Syria was Mu'awiyah of the Meccan house of the Umayyads. He used the country as a base for expeditions

Great Mosque of Damascus

Great Mosque of Damascus, interior view of the courtyard. Nasser Rabbat

The Great Mosque of Damascus (also called the Umayyad Mosque) is the earliest surviving stone mosque, built between 705 and 715 CE by the Umayyad caliph al-Walīd I. The mosque stands on the site of a 1st-century Hellenic temple to Jupiter and of a later church of St. John the Baptist. Some Syrio-Roman fragments remain in the structure, as does a shrine supposedly enclosing a relic honoured by Muslims as well as Christians, the head of St. John the Baptist.

The mosque occupies a huge quadrangle 515 by 330 feet (157 by 100 m) and contains a large open courtyard surrounded by an arcade of arches supported by slender columns. The *liwan,* or hall of worship, running the length of the south side of the mosque, is divided into three long aisles by rows of columns and arches. A transept with a central octagonal dome, originally wooden, cuts across the aisles at their midpoint. The marble grilles that cover the windows in the south wall are the earliest example of geometric interlace in Islamic architecture. The walls of the mosque were once covered with more than an acre of mosaics depicting a fanciful landscape thought to be the Qu'rānic paradise, but only fragments survive. The mosque was destroyed by Timur in 1401, rebuilt by the Arabs, and damaged by fire in 1893. Although it could not be restored to its original splendour, the mosque is still an impressive architectural monument.

against the Byzantine Empire, for this purpose building the first Muslim navy in the Mediterranean. When civil war broke out in the Muslim Empire, as a result of the murder of 'Uthmān and the nomination of 'Alī as caliph, Syria stood firm behind Mu'awiyah, who extended his authority over neighbouring provinces and was proclaimed caliph in 660. He was the first of the Umayyad line, which ruled the empire, with Syria as its core and Damascus its capital, for almost a century.

The Umayyads

The early Umayyad period was one of strength and expansion. The army, mainly Arab and largely Syrian, extended the frontiers of Islam. It carried the war against Byzantium into Asia Minor and besieged Constantinople; eastward it penetrated into Khorasan, Turkistan, and northwestern India; and, spreading along the northern coast of Africa, it occupied much of Spain. This vast empire was given a regular administration that gradually acquired an Arab Muslim character. Syrians played an important part in it, and the country profited from the wealth pouring from the rich provinces to the empire's centre. The caliphs built splendid palaces and the first great monuments of Muslim religious architecture: the Dome of the Rock in Jerusalem and the Great Mosque of Damascus, constructed by the Umayyads. The religious sciences of Islam began to develop, while Christian culture still flourished. Except under 'Umar II Christians were treated with favour, and there were Christian officials at court.

Under the later Umayyads the strength of the central government declined. There were factions and feuds inside the ruling group: the Arabs of Iraq resented the domination of Syria; the non-Arab converts to Islam (*mawālī*) resented the social gap between them and the Arabs; and devout Muslims regarded the Umayyads as too worldly in their lives and policies. After the defeat and death of ʿAlī's son Ḥusayn at the Battle of Karbalāʾ in 680, sentiment in favour of the family of ʿAlī was still strong. The later Umayyads could not control these discontents. Their rule was finally overthrown and the family virtually destroyed by the new ʿAbbāsid dynasty in 750. Among these was ʿAbd al-Raḥmān, a member of the ruling family, who survived the assault and fled westward to reestablish the Umayyads in Al-Andalus.

The ʿAbbāsids

The end of the Umayyad dynasty meant a shift in power from Syria to Iraq. Syria became a dependent province of the caliphate. Its loyalty was suspect, for Umayyad sentiment lingered on, and the last pro-Umayyad revolt was not crushed until 905. The Christian population was treated with less favour. Discriminatory legislation was applied to it under some caliphs, and the process of conversion to Islam went on. Closely connected with it was the gradual adoption of Arabic in place of Greek and Aramaic, although the latter survived in a few villages.

From the 9th to the 12th Century

As the ʿAbbāsid dynasty disintegrated in its turn, Syria drifted out of the sphere of influence of Baghdad. In 877 it was annexed by the Ṭūlūnid dynasty of Egypt, and this began a political connection that was to last with intervals for more than six centuries. In northern Syria the Ṭūlūnids were succeeded by a local Arab dynasty, the Ḥamdānids of Aleppo, founded by Sayf al-Dawlah (ruled 944–967). They engaged in war with Byzantium, in which their early successes were followed by the Greek recovery of Antioch (969). In central and southern Syria another Egyptian dynasty, the Ikhshīdids, established themselves (941–969). Their successors, the Fāṭimid caliphs of Cairo, later absorbed the whole country.

In spite of political disturbances, the 10th and 11th centuries were a period of flourishing culture. Around the court of the Ḥamdānids lived some of the greatest Arabic writers: the poets al-Mutanabbī and al-Maʿarrī, the philosopher al-Fārābī, and the anthologist Abū al-Faraj al-Iṣbāhanī. It was a period of ferment in Islamic thought, when the challenge to Sunni Islam from Shīʿism and its offshoots reached its height. The Fāṭimids were themselves Shīʿites. At the end of the 10th century, Syria was threatened by the Qarmatians, adherents of an extreme form of Shīʿism who had established a state in the Persian Gulf. The danger was beaten back, but it returned as an esoteric doctrine spread by the Ismāʿīlīs from their centre at Salamiyyah in northern Syria.

In the second half of the 11th century Syria fell into the hands of the Seljuq Turks, who had established a sultanate in Asia Minor. They occupied Aleppo and then Damascus. But after the death of the sultan Malik-Shāh in 1092 the Seljuq Empire fell to pieces, and between 1098 and 1124 the Crusaders occupied Antioch, Jerusalem, Al-Karak in Transjordan, and the coast.

The Crusaders organized their conquests into four states owing allegiance to the king of Jerusalem. Their situation was precarious. The Crusaders were always a minority in their states, and they never penetrated far into the interior. They could maintain their position only so long as the Muslim states surrounding were weak and divided. Zangī, the Turkish ruler of Mosul, occupied Aleppo in 1128 and recovered Edessa from the Crusaders in 1144. His son Nūr al-Dīn united inner Syria and annexed Egypt. After his death his kingdom was rebuilt and strengthened by his viceroy in Egypt, Saladin, who ended Fāṭimid rule, created a strong kingdom of Egypt and Syria, and defeated the Crusaders at the great Battle of Ḥaṭṭīn (1187). He recovered all of Palestine and most of the inland strongholds of the Crusaders. Soon afterward, however, the Third Crusade recaptured part of the coast.

The Ayyūbids and Mamlūks

After Saladin's death his kingdom was split up among members of his family, the Ayyūbids, who established principalities in Aleppo, Ḥamāh, Ḥimṣ, Damascus, Ba'labakk (Baalbek), and Transjordan and ruled them until 1260. The period of Nūr al-Dīn, Saladin, and their successors was of great importance. Owing largely to the establishment of Italian trading centres on the coast and better security, economic life recovered and Syria reached a level of prosperity such as it had not enjoyed for centuries. The Ayyūbid rulers stimulated culture and architecture. Following the Seljuqs, they created a new land system based on the grant of rights over land in return for military service. They were champions of Sunni Islam against the Shī'ite sects that had gained ground in the previous era. They built colleges of a new type, the madrasah, as centres of learning. Their efforts to stamp out Shī'ite sects were not completely successful. The Nizārīs (Assassins), a subsect of the Ismā'īlīs, kept their strongholds in the mountains and had some political importance.

Although strong internally, the state was still in danger from the Bedouin tribes of the desert and from the Mongols, who invaded Syria for the first time in 1260 and sacked Aleppo. They were driven back not by the local rulers but by a new Egyptian military power, the Mamlūks, a self-perpetuating elite of slaves and freedmen, mainly of Turkish and Circassian origin, who had replaced the Ayyūbids as rulers of Egypt in 1250. In 1260 they defeated the Mongols at the Battle of 'Ayn Jālūt in Palestine. The victorious Mamlūk general, Baybars I, made himself sultan of a reunited kingdom of Syria and Egypt, which he ruled until his death in 1277. This state continued to exist for more than two centuries. In 1291 it won back Acre and other coastal towns from the Crusaders, who were expelled. A few years later it took the last Crusading stronghold, the island of Ruad (Arwād). The Mamlūks reorganized the Ayyūbid principalities as six provinces, of which Damascus was the largest and most important. Political power was in the hands of the Mamlūk elite, who held land in virtual ownership in return for military service in the cavalry. But there was a local element in the government, the civil servants being drawn mainly from Syrian Arab families with their tradition of religious learning.

Like the Ayyūbids, the Mamlūks favoured Sunni Islam. Religious culture flourished and produced a number of great scholars, such as the Ḥanbalī jurist Ibn Taymiyyah. For religious and political reasons, the Mamlūks dealt severely with the religious minorities living in the coastal mountain ranges: Druze, Maronite Christians, Ismāʿīlīs, and 'Alawites. One of the principal reasons for this severity was the Mamlūks' fear that these minorities might cooperate with the Crusaders, should they attempt to return.

In the early Mamlūk period, Syria remained prosperous. The rulers constructed public works, and Venetian merchants carried on their coastal trade. But in 1401 came a blow to economic life: a new Mongol invader, Timur (Tamerlane), sacked Aleppo and Damascus. His empire did not long survive his death in 1405, but the damage had been done. The cities had been burned, a large part of their population killed, and many craftsmen taken away to Central Asia.

OTTOMAN PERIOD

Throughout the 15th century, Mamlūk Syria continued to decline, while a new power was growing to the north, that of the Ottoman Turkish sultanate in Asia Minor. Having occupied Constantinople and the Balkans, it began to look southward. In 1516 Sultan Selim I defeated the Mamlūks in the Battle of Marj Dābiq and occupied the whole of Syria that year and Egypt the next.

Ottoman Government, 16th–17th Centuries

Although parts of Syria enjoyed some local autonomy, the area as a whole remained for 400 years an integral section of the Ottoman Empire. It was divided into provinces, each under a governor: Damascus, Aleppo, and later Tripoli and Ṣaydā, or Sidon, of which the administrative centre was later moved to Acre. Damascus, the largest, had special importance as the place from which the pilgrimage to Mecca was organized every year. The governor of Damascus led the pilgrimage when possible, and most of the revenues of the province were earmarked for its expenses.

The tax system continued in principle to be that of Muslim law—a land tax, a poll tax on Christians and Jews, and customs duties. But the Ottomans, like their predecessors, gave the right to collect and keep the land tax in return for military service. Later this system was allowed to decay, and tax collection was turned over to tax farmers (*mültezim*), who became in the course of time nearly a landowning class. The official religious hierarchy of judges, jurisconsults, and preachers served as an intermediary between government and subjects, as did guild masters and the heads of the local mystical orders (Sufis).

Within this framework of law, order, and taxation, the local communities were left to regulate their own lives. In the desert, the Bedouin tribes were controlled to some extent by gifts, the encouragement of factions, and occasional military expeditions but otherwise were not interfered with. The ʿAlawites and the Ismāʿīlīs dwelling in the Al-Anṣariyyah Mountains were watched by the Ottoman governors, but they were not interfered with so long as they paid their taxes. In the Jabal Al-Durūz region, south of Damascus, there grew up an autonomous community of Druze farmers who did not pay taxes to the Ottoman authorities. The authority of the Christian patriarchs over their communities was recognized. In the community of scholars called the ulama (Arabic: ʿ*ulamāʾ*), most positions except the highest were held by members of local families having a tradition of religious learning. They continued to be, as under the Mamlūks, spokesmen and leaders of the Muslim citizens.

The early Ottoman governors paid much attention to agriculture, and their fiscal system was designed to encourage it. In parts of Syria it flourished during the 16th and 17th centuries, and, apart from cereals for local consumption, cotton and silk were produced for export. Aleppo and Damascus not only were important centres of handicrafts but also served as market towns for the desert and countryside and as stages on the desert routes to the Persian Gulf and Persia. Aleppo also was an important centre of trade with Europe; French and English merchants had largely replaced Italian ones, and there grew up also a class of Syrian Christian and

'Abd al-Ghanī al-Nābulusī

(b. March 19, 1641, Damascus—d. March 5, 1731)

'Abd al-Ghanī al-Nābulusī was a Syrian mystic prose and verse writer on the cultural and religious thought of his time.

Orphaned at an early age, 'Abd al-Ghanī joined the Islamic mystical orders of the Qādiriyyah and the Naqshbandiyyah. He then spent seven years in isolation in his house, studying the mystics on their expression of divine experiences. 'Abd al-Ghanī traveled extensively throughout the Islamic world, visiting Istanbul in 1664, Lebanon in 1688, Jerusalem and Palestine in 1689, Egypt and Arabia in 1693, and Tripoli in 1700.

His more than 200 written works can be divided into three categories: Sufism; travel accounts; and miscellaneous subjects, including poetry, eulogies, correspondence, prophecy, the interpretation of dreams, and the question of the lawfulness of the use of tobacco. The main component in his original Sufi writing, as distinguished from his commentaries on the works of others, is the concept of *waḥdat al-wujūd* ("divine existential unity" of God and the universe and, hence, of man). His travel accounts are considered by many scholars to be the most important of his writings; the descriptions of his journeys provide vital information on the customs, beliefs, and practices of the peoples and places he visited.

Jewish merchants who developed contacts with Egypt, Italy, and France.

Throughout the 17th and 18th centuries, the position of the Christians improved. Catholic missions, protected by France, enlarged the Catholic communities of both Latin and Eastern rites, founded schools, and spread knowledge of European languages. Colleges in Rome produced an educated priesthood, and the Christian communities in Aleppo and Lebanon brought forth scholars. Muslim Arab culture of the time produced the theologian

ʿAbd al-Ghanī al-Nābulusī, as well as Ibrāhīm al-Ḥalabī, a systematic jurist.

Decline of Ottoman Authority

In spite of widespread unrest in the early 17th century, Ottoman rule was in general stable and effective until the end of that century. After that it declined rapidly, in Syria as elsewhere. Control by the central government weakened; the standard of administration sank; and the Janissaries (the elite troops of the sultan) lost their discipline and became a menace to order. The result was a shrinkage of agricultural production, as the villages suffered from the depredations of soldiery and tax collectors and from Bedouin incursions. This was a period of activity in the Syrian desert, and Bedouin tribes, moving northwest from Arabia, extended their control far into the settled land. In the towns there was also a decline. The desert routes were unsafe, and the European merchant colonies were shrinking. But there was still a vigorous commercial life. The standard of craftsmanship was high, and the great tradition of Islamic architecture was continued under the patronage of provincial dignitaries and governors.

Ottoman authority did reassert itself to some extent, but in a new form. For most of the 18th century, Damascus was ruled by governors belonging to the ʿAẓm family, loyal to the sultan but with more independence than earlier sultans would have allowed. They controlled the Janissaries, kept back the Bedouin, maintained security, and sometimes extended their authority to other provinces. In the province of Sidon, power was held on similar terms by a ruthless and able Bosnian governor, Aḥmad al-Jazzār (ruled 1775–1804), and his group of Mamlūks. Such rulers raised their own armies, but this involved additional taxation and further depressed the condition of the peasants. Agriculture flourished in the hilly districts, which were virtually beyond Ottoman control, free from Bedouin attacks, and overseen by strong local rulers who protected agriculture and made Acre a prosperous centre of trade.

At the beginning of the 19th century, Syria had some islands of prosperity: Aleppo and Damascus (each with roughly 100,000 inhabitants), Mount Lebanon, and certain other secluded districts. In general, however, the country was in decay, the small towns subsisting on local trade and the villagers receding in face of the Bedouin. The Ottoman hold on the country was at its weakest. In Damascus and Aleppo the governors were scarcely able to control the population of city or countryside. The prince of Lebanon, Bashīr II (ruled 1788–1840), who had been installed by al-Jazzār and remained quiet while al-Jazzār was alive, gradually extended his control over districts beyond Lebanon. In 1810 the Wahhābīs from central Arabia threatened Damascus.

Egyptian Domination

In 1831 the ruler of Egypt, Muḥammad ʿAlī, sent his son Ibrāhīm Pasha at the head of his modern army into Palestine. Helped by Bashīr and other local leaders, Ibrāhīm conquered the country and advanced into Asia Minor. He ruled Syria for almost 10 years. The whole country was controlled from Damascus. There and in the provincial centres the governors were Egyptians, but they were assisted by councils representing the population. In political matters Ibrāhīm relied largely on Bashīr. New taxes were introduced and strictly collected, agriculture was encouraged, and the Bedouin pushed back. After an abortive attempt to introduce trade monopolies, Ibrāhīm encouraged European traders by maintaining better security. The Christian and Jewish populations were treated with consideration.

After a time, Ibrāhīm's rule became unpopular because his taxes were heavy and because he tried to disarm and conscript the population. The European powers (except France) also objected to Egyptian rule in Syria because it was a threat to the Ottoman Empire, the weakness or disintegration of which might cause a European crisis. In 1839 war broke out between Muḥammad 'Alī and his suzerain, the sultan. Ibrāhīm defeated the Ottoman army, but in 1840 the European powers intervened. After an ultimatum, a British, Ottoman, and Austrian force landed on the Syrian coast. The British encouraged a local insurrection, and the Egyptians were forced to withdraw from Syria, which reverted to the sultan's government.

Ottoman Rule Restored

The next 20 years were a period of mounting crises. Lebanon became the scene of a struggle for power between Druzes and Maronites, with undertones of social conflict. In Syria an attempt was made to apply the new Ottoman administrative system. But the new system of taxation and conscription caused unrest. This situation was worsened by the growth of European influence. The Muslim majority became aware of Ottoman vulnerability to European aggression, and the connection of France with the Catholics and of Russia with the Orthodox both encouraged the minorities to hope for a more favourable position and focused on them the hostility of their Muslim compatriots. There was also economic unrest. European goods flooded the market and replaced some of the products of local craftsmen. This diminished the prosperity of the artisan class, largely Muslim, but increased that of the import merchants, mainly Christians and Jews.

The tension thus generated burst forth in 1860, when a civil war of Druzes and Maronites in Lebanon touched off a massacre of Christians by Muslims in Damascus. The Ottoman government sent a special commissioner to punish the guilty and suppress disorder, and to firmly establish Istanbul's authority. France sent an expeditionary force, and a European commission discussed the future of the country, coming to the conclusion that Lebanon (the mountain itself but not the coastal towns) should be an autonomous district (*mutaṣarrifiyyah*) but that no change should be made in Syria.

From then until the collapse of the Ottoman Empire, Syria continued to be governed as a group of Ottoman provinces. From 1888 there were three: Damascus, Aleppo, and Beirut. The new administrative and legal system was more carefully applied, and a new type of educated official gradually raised its standards. The introduction of railways and telegraphs made possible a stricter control. A French-built railway linked Beirut and Damascus, with a later extension running north to Aleppo, and in 1908 the Hejaz Railway was opened to take pilgrims from Damascus to Medina. Railways and better security encouraged agriculture. Aleppo (population about 200,000) and Damascus (250,000) both had a flourishing trade, but the crafts declined, and the desert routes suffered from the opening of the Suez Canal.

In the cities there was a considerable change in social life. The upper and middle classes adopted the clothes and social customs of western Europe, and Western-style schools flourished. In 1866 the American Protestant Mission opened in Beirut the Syrian Protestant College (later the American University of Beirut), and in 1881 the

French Jesuits opened the Université Saint-Joseph in the same town. The Ottoman government opened schools, and young men of the great Arab families of the towns began to attend the higher schools in Constantinople and to go on to civil or military service.

Under Sultan Abdülhamid II (ruled 1876–1909) the Muslim Arabs of Syria were reasonably content. Syrian Arabs played a leading part at the sultan's court and Abdülhamid lavished patronage on Sufi orders. His emphasis on Islamic solidarity fostered obedience to the sultan as a religious duty. There also appeared a dissident current of Salafi Islamic reform allied to the Ottoman constitutional movement. The Salafis favoured a return to pristine Islam as a way to purify ritual and allow flexible adaptation to modern political and technological advances.

After the Young Turk revolution of 1908, relations between Arabs and Turks grew worse. Power fell into the hands of a Turkish military group whose policy stimulated the growth of opposition. Arab nationalist and Syrian patriotic feeling became more conscious, and political parties, both open and secret, were organized by Syrians in Cairo, Constantinople, and Paris, as well as in Syria itself.

World War I

When the Ottoman Empire entered World War I in 1914, Syria became a military base. In 1915 an Ottoman army under German command attacked the British position on the Suez Canal, and from 1916 a British and imperial force based in Egypt, with a French contingent, undertook the invasion of Palestine. By the end of 1917 General Sir Edmund (later Field Marshal Viscount) Allenby had occupied Jerusalem, and by November 1918 his troops had taken Syria. Most Christians and Jews

Fayṣal I

(b. May 20, 1885, Mecca—d. September 8, 1933, Bern, Switzerland)

Fayṣal was an Arab statesman and king of Iraq (1921–33) who was a leader in advancing Arab nationalism during and after World War I.

Fayṣal was the son of Ḥusayn ibn 'Alī, emir and grand *sharīf* of Mecca who ruled the Hejaz from 1916 to 1924. When World War I provided an opportunity for rebellion for many Arab leaders who had come to resent Ottoman rule, including certain Syrian Arabs who looked to Ḥusayn for leadership because he was not under direct Ottoman rule, Fayṣal in 1915 travelled to Damascus to reach an understanding with the secret Arab nationalist societies there about the terms under which they would support an Arab revolt led by Ḥusayn. Fayṣal's ability to meet with diverse groups previously unknown to him and to win their recognition of Ḥusayn as an Arab leader indicated the existence of a nascent Arab nationalism.

When in the following year the Arab revolt was declared, Fayṣal played an important part in the military campaigns against the Ottomans. An Arab military force occupied Damascus in September 1918, and Fayṣal was declared king of Syria in accord with his understanding that Arab support for British military ambitions would be rewarded by British support for the creation of an Arab state consisting of most of Syria. When Fayṣal went to Paris in 1919 to participate in the peace conference, however, he became clearly aware of French determination to establish a sphere of influence in Lebanon and Syria. Realizing that he would have to make concessions, he negotiated the agreement accepting French military occupation of Lebanon and the Syrian coastal regions as far north as Alexandretta (modern Iskenderun, Turkey). In January 1920 he returned to Damascus, where he was unable to calm the violent resentment aroused by the news of French pretensions. Most Arab leaders did not understand the futility of resisting French military power and the consequent pressures under which he had laboured in Paris. When France soon found reason to invade Fayṣal's kingdom and occupy Damascus (July 1920), Fayṣal himself was forced into exile, eventually going to London at the invitation of the British government.

Meanwhile, Britain had established a sphere of influence in Iraq. To ease resistance to British rule, Britain decided in March 1921 to sponsor Fayṣal as king of an Iraqi government with which Britain would conclude a treaty providing for eventual independence. Fayṣal accepted the plan and was enthusiastically welcomed in Iraq, where he was crowned in August 1921. His ability to command widespread support in Iraq as well as Syria provided a continuing indication of nationalistic feeling among Arabs of the entire Fertile Crescent. Indeed, as a Pan-Arab leader he had no specific political roots in Iraq, deriving his authority by moderating various conflicting elements. He valued British friendship while maintaining his full credentials among fervent Arab nationalists as their leader. From his position of influence, he negotiated with Britain a series of treaties culminating in 1930 with a treaty that enabled Iraq to achieve complete independence and membership in the League of Nations by 1932.

welcomed the occupation. Among the Muslims a large proportion had remained loyal to the empire, as being all that was left of the political independence of Islam, but the nationalist societies had made common cause with the ruler of the Hejaz, Sharīf Ḥusayn, forming an alliance with Britain against their Turkish suzerain. An Arab army under the command of Ḥusayn's son Fayṣal was formed in the Hejaz, with Syrian and other Arab officers and British help led by T. E. Lawrence. It took part, under Allenby's general command, in the Syrian campaign helping to capture Damascus.

When the war ended, Allenby installed an Arab military administration, under Fayṣal, in Damascus and the interior. The French took over the coast, with Beirut as their centre, and the British took over Palestine. There followed several unsettled years while the fate of Syria was being decided. During the war the British government had made promises, to Ḥusayn and other Arab leaders, that the Arabs would be independent in those countries that they helped to liberate, subject to certain reservations, the precise extent of which has never been clear. Then, in November 1918, Britain and France declared their intention of establishing in Syria and Iraq "national governments drawing their authority from the initiative and free choice of the native populations."

By the Sykes-Picot Agreement of 1916, France was to be free to establish its administration in Lebanon and on the coast and to provide advice and assistance to whatever regime existed in the interior. In March 1920 a Syrian Congress meeting in Damascus elected Fayṣal king of a united Syria including Palestine. But in April the Allied Conference of San Remo decided that both should be placed under the new mandate system and that France should have the mandate for Syria.

FRENCH MANDATE

In June 1920 a French ultimatum demanding Syrian recognition of the mandate was followed by a French occupation and the expulsion in July of Fayṣal. In July 1922 the League of Nations approved the texts of the French Mandate for Syria and Lebanon. Lebanon had already, in August 1920, been declared a separate state, with the addition of Beirut, Tripoli, and certain other districts, to the prewar autonomous province. Politically, "Syria" henceforth acquired a narrower meaning; it referred to what was left of geographical Syria once Transjordan, Lebanon, and Palestine had been detached from it.

The mandate placed on France the responsibility of creating and controlling an administration, developing the resources of the country, and preparing it for self-government. A number of local governments were set up: one for the Al-Anṣariyyah Mountains region, where the majority belonged to the 'Alawite sect, one for the Jabal

Al-Durūz region, where most of the inhabitants were Druzes, and eventually one for the rest of Syria, with its capital at Damascus.

The French mandatory administration carried out much constructive work. Roads were built; town planning was carried out and urban amenities were improved; land tenure was reformed in some districts; and agriculture was encouraged, particularly in the fertile Al-Jazīrah. The University of Damascus was established, with its teaching being mainly in Arabic.

It was more difficult to prepare Syria for self-government because of the difference between French and Syrian conceptions of what was implied. Most French officials and statesmen thought in terms of a long period of control. Further, they did not wish to hand over power to the Muslim majority in a way that might persuade their Christian protégés that they were giving up France's traditional policy of protecting the Christians of the Levant. In Syria, many members of the minorities and a smaller proportion of the majority wanted the French to remain as a help in constructing a modern society and government. The greater part of the urban population, however, and in particular the educated elite, wanted Syria to be independent and to include Lebanon, Palestine, and Transjordan, if possible, and certainly the Druze and 'Alawite districts.

The first crisis in Franco-Syrian relations came in 1925, when a revolt in Jabal Al-Durūz, sparked by local grievances, led to an alliance between the Druze rebels and the nationalists of Damascus, newly organized in the People's Party. For a time the rebels controlled much of the countryside. In October 1925, bands entered the city of Damascus itself, and this led to a two-day bombardment by the French. The revolt did not subside completely until 1927, but even before the end of 1925 the French had started a policy of conciliation. In 1928 elections were held for a Constituent Assembly. The nationalists won the election and took office in a new government. The assembly drafted a constitution, but their draft was not wholly acceptable to the high commissioner, because it spoke of the unity of geographical Syria and did not explicitly safeguard the French position of control.

In May 1930 the high commissioner dissolved the assembly and enacted the constitution with certain changes. There followed unsuccessful negotiations for a Franco-Syrian treaty, but in 1936 the advent of the Popular Front government in France changed the situation. Negotiations took place with the nationalists, now organized in the National Bloc. A treaty was signed in September 1936. It provided for Syrian independence, Franco-Syrian consultation on foreign policy, French priority in advice and assistance, and the retention by France of two military bases. The Druze and ʿAlawite districts were to be incorporated into Syria but not Lebanon, with which France signed a similar treaty in November. A Parliament was elected; the leader of the Bloc, Hāshim al-ʿAtāsī, was chosen as president of the republic; and a nationalist government took office.

The Syrian government ratified the treaty before the end of 1936, but France never did so. When Turkey put forward claims to Alexandretta, where Turks were the largest element in the mixed population, France found it advisable, for strategic reasons, to yield to its demands. In 1937 the district (later given the Turkish name of Hatay) was granted an autonomous status; in 1939 it was incorporated into Turkey.

By the end of 1938 it was clear that the French government had no intention of ratifying the treaty. In July 1939 the president and government resigned, and the constitution was suspended.

WORLD WAR II AND INDEPENDENCE

In June 1940, after the Franco-German armistice, the French in Syria announced that they would cease hostilities against Germany and Italy and recognize the Vichy government. Political uncertainty and the growing scarcity of goods and rising prices caused unrest, which was led by one of the prominent nationalists, Shukri al-Quwatli. In May 1941 the Vichy government allowed German aircraft to land and refuel en route to Iraq, and in June, British, Commonwealth, and Free French forces invaded Syria. French troops resisted for a month, but Damascus was occupied on June 21, and hostilities ceased at midnight on July 11–12.

From then until 1946, Syria was jointly occupied by British and French forces. At the moment of invasion, the Free French had proclaimed Syrian and Lebanese independence, and this was underwritten by the British government, which recognized French predominance in Syria and Lebanon, provided France carry out its promise of independence. In the interests of its Arab policy, Britain used its position of strength to persuade the Free French to carry out their undertaking. Elections held in 1943 resulted in a nationalist victory, and Shukri al-Quwatli became president of the republic.

There followed two years of disagreement about the transfer of authority from the French administration to the Syrian and Lebanese governments. A crisis took place in 1945, when the French refusal to transfer control of the local armed forces led to disorders, culminating in a

French bombardment of Damascus and British intervention. After long negotiations and discussion in the UN Security Council, agreement was reached on simultaneous British and French withdrawal from Syria and Lebanon. Withdrawal from Syria was completed by April 1946. Syria had already become a founder member of the UN and of the Arab League.

EARLY YEARS OF INDEPENDENCE

The humiliating failure of the Arab intervention in Palestine against the newly created State of Israel in May 1948 brought serious discredit to the governments of the Arab countries involved, but nowhere more than in Syria.

Fundamental to the Syrian problem was the ethnically, religiously, and socially heterogeneous nature of the emerging republic. The new state united the ʿAlawite and Druze territories, which had formerly enjoyed separate status, with the predominantly Sunni regions of Damascus, Ḥimṣ, Ḥamāh, and Aleppo. The ʿAlawites and Druzes formed compact communities in their respective regions. Throughout the country, and particularly in the cities, there were large communities of Christians.

In addition to this religious heterogeneity, there was an equally important social heterogeneity. Syria's population was composed of townspeople, peasants, and nomads, three groups with little in common. Economic differences added further complexity. In the cities the ostentatious wealth of the notables contrasted sharply with the poverty of the masses. Those same notables were also the owners of large agricultural estates on which the peasants were practically serfs. It was the Sunni landowning notables who led the resistance to the French. When Syria achieved independence, they took power and endeavoured to forge a unitary state. They proved unequal to the task.

By 1949 the small but rising middle class, among which new social ideas were developing, and minorities, who resented the growing threat to their particularism, were increasingly opposed to the government. The rulers, having tasted power after so long a struggle for independence, refused those concessions that might have saved them. Moreover, they appeared to be more devoted to achieving Pan-Arab goals than to solving the problems closer to home. In the years immediately following World War II, Iraq and Saudi Arabia were making rival bids for Pan-Arab leadership. The ruling National Bloc in Syria readily divided into two new parties: a National Party headed by Shukri al-Quwatli, which represented the business interests of the Damascus notables and supported Saudi Arabia; and a resuscitated People's Party, which represented the interests of the Aleppo notables and supported Iraq. The socialist and secular Arab nationalist Ba'th Party was recruiting followers among students and army officers, winning support particularly among the 'Alawite and other minorities that were strongly represented among the younger officers of the army.

The Colonels

The short-lived civilian order in Syria ended in March 1949, when Colonel Husni al-Za'im overthrew the Quwatli government in a bloodless coup. Za'im was himself overthrown in August by Colonel Sami al-Hinnawi. A third coup, led by Colonel Adib al-Shishakli, followed in December, and in November 1951 Shishakli removed his associates by a fourth coup.

The military dictators of Syria were officers of no particular ideological commitment, and the regimes they led may be described as conservative. All ruled in association with veteran politicians. Among the politically minded army officers at the time, many were Pan-Arabist Ba'th Socialists. Opposing the Ba'th officers were officers of a radically different political persuasion, who followed the Syrian Social Nationalist Party (SSNP; the Parti Populaire Syrien), an authoritarian party devoted to the establishment of a Pan-Syrian national state.

Shishakli was overthrown in February 1954 by a military coup led by Colonel Faysal al-Atasi, and Parliament was restored. The SSNP forthwith lost its influence in Syrian politics and in the following year was suppressed in the army. From that time the Ba'thists in the army had no serious rival. Changes in agriculture took place in the 1950s, separate from the struggle for control of the state, and they had an important effect on the lives of many people. Capital-intensive cotton production grew rapidly in the newly planted lands of the northeast.

The Union with Egypt, 1958–61

The years that followed the overthrow of Shishakli in Syria saw the rise of President Gamal Abdel Nasser of Egypt to leadership of the Pan-Arab unity movement. The coalition regime in Syria turned more and more to Egypt for support and also established the first friendly contacts with the communist countries. In February 1958 Syria, under the leadership of the Ba'th Party, gave up its sovereignty to become, for the next three and a half years, the "Northern Province" of the United Arab Republic (UAR), of which Nasser was president.

The union of Syria with Egypt proved a bitter disappointment, for the Egyptians tended to treat the Syrians as subordinates. Tensions were heightened when drought damaged Syria's economy. In September 1961 a coup led by Syrian army officers reestablished Syria as an independent state.

The "Secessionist" Regime, 1961–63

The coup of 1961 paved the way for a return of the old class of notables to power as parliamentary elections were held. The "secessionist" regime, though civilian at the surface, was still under army control, and in the army the Baʿth was powerful. The regime made hardly any concessions to the socialism of the Baʿth and the pro-Nasser Pan-Arabists. The secessionist regime set out quickly to undo the socialist measures introduced under the union with Egypt (such as land reforms and the nationalization of large business enterprises), thus playing into the hands of the Baʿth.

BAʿTHIST SYRIA AFTER 1963

In March 1963 Baʿthist supporters in the army seized power. From 1963 through the early 21st century, Syria remained continuously under Baʿth rule, most notably under Ḥafiz al-Assad, who came to power in the early 1970s and served as president of Syria for some three decades.

Emergence and Fracture of the Syrian Baʿth

A month before the Baʿth coup in Syria, the Iraqi branch of the party had seized power in Baghdad. A Baʿthist union between Syria and Iraq seemed imminent, but it was opposed by the pro-Nasser Arab unionists in Damascus and Baghdad. The Baʿth leaders of Iraq and Syria flew to Cairo for unity talks with President Nasser, but Nasser would agree to a union only on his own terms, and the

Ḥafiz al-Assad

(b. October 6, 1930, Qardāḥa, Syria—d. June 10, 2000, Damascus)

As president of Syria (1971–2000), Ḥafiz al-Assad brought stability to the country and established it as a powerful presence in the Middle East.

Assad was born into a poor ʿAlawite family and joined the Syrian wing of the Baʿth Party in 1946 as a student activist. In 1952 he entered the Ḥimṣ Military Academy, graduating three years later as an air force pilot. While exiled to Egypt (1959–61) during Syria's short-lived union with Egypt in the United Arab Republic, Assad and other military officers formed a committee to resurrect the fortunes of the Syrian Baʿth Party. After the Baʿthists took power in 1963, Assad became commander of the air force. In 1966, after taking part in a coup that overthrew the civilian leadership of the party and sent its founders into exile, he became minister of defense. During Assad's ministry Syria lost the Golan Heights to Israel in the June (Six-Day) War in 1967, dealing Assad a blow that shaped much of his future political career. Assad then engaged in a protracted power struggle with Salah al-Jadid—chief of staff of the armed forces, Assad's political mentor, and effective leader of Syria—until finally in November 1970 Assad seized control, arresting Jadid and other members of the government. He became prime minister and in 1971 was elected president.

Assad set about building up the Syrian military with Soviet aid and gaining the loyalty of the Syrian populace with public works funded by Arab donors and international lending institutions. Political dissenters were eliminated by arrest, torture, and execution, and when the Muslim Brotherhood mounted a rebellion in Ḥamāh in 1982, Assad ruthlessly suppressed it at a cost of some 20,000 lives and the near-destruction of the city. In foreign affairs Assad tried to establish Syria as a leader of the Arab world. A new alliance with Egypt culminated in a surprise attack on Israel in October 1973, but Egypt's unexpected cessation of hostilities exposed Syria to military defeat and earned Egypt's president, Anwar el-Sādāt, Assad's enduring resentment. In 1976, with Lebanon racked by a bloody civil war, Assad dispatched several divisions to that country and secured their permanent presence there as part of a peacekeeping force sponsored by the Arab

League. After Israel's invasion and occupation of southern Lebanon in 1982–85, Assad was able to reassert control of the country, eventually compelling Lebanese Christians to accept constitutional changes granting Muslims equal representation in the government. Assad also apparently aided radical Palestinian and Muslim terrorist groups based in Lebanon and Syria.

His rivalry with the Iraqi wing of the Ba'th Party underlay Assad's long-standing enmity toward the Iraqi leader Ṣaddām Ḥussein. Assad supported Iran in its war against Iraq (1980–88), and he readily joined the U.S.-led alliance against Iraq in the Persian Gulf War of 1990–91. This cooperation resulted in more cordial relations with Western governments, which previously had condemned his sponsoring of terrorism. Assad sought to establish peaceful relations with Israel in the mid-1990s, but his repeated call for the return of the Golan Heights stalled the talks. In 1998 he cultivated closer ties with Iraq in light of Israel's growing strategic partnership with Turkey.

talks failed. In Syria the pro-Nasser Arab unionists were expelled from the coalition, and an exclusively Ba'th regime was established.

The Ba'thists in Syria were soon faced with a serious problem. Although their party in Syria was led by Syrians, it also promoted Pan-Arabism and had branches in Iraq, Lebanon, and Jordan. The continued subordination of the Syrian branch of the party to the Pan-Arab central committee gave non-Syrian Ba'thists a say in Syrian affairs. As a result, the Syrian Ba'thists established their own Pan-Arab central committee, thereby creating a deadly rivalry with the Iraqi Ba'thists, as each claimed to be the legitimate leader of the Pan-Arab nationalist cause.

With 'Alawite military officers in control, the Syrian Ba'th Party crushed domestic opposition by setting up a police state and by appealing to the middle- and lower-class residents of small towns and villages, who had long

The Golan Heights became part of Syria after World War I, but in 1967 an assault by Israeli armed forces placed the heights under Israeli military control. In 1981 Israel unilaterally annexed the area. David Furst/AFP/ Getty Images

resented the power of the politicians and large landowners in Damascus and Aleppo. Rivalry within the Baʿth Party led to a coup d'état in February 1966 that installed a faction headed by Colonel Salah al-Jadid. The neo-Baʿth regime pursued more radical foreign and domestic policies. By 1969 the party was divided between a mostly civilian wing, led by Jadid, and a mostly military wing, led by Gen. Ḥafiz al-Assad. The latter seized power in November 1970 and was sworn in as president on March 14, 1971. He was subsequently reelected with no opposition on several occasions, including a referendum on December 2, 1991.

Baʿthist authoritarian rule enjoyed some popularity because it enacted policies that favoured economic development, land reform, promotion of education, strengthening of the military, and vehement opposition to Israel. As these policies took effect, nationalists, peasants, and workers came to support the Assad regime. In contrast to the chaos of political life from 1945 to 1963, Syria experienced remarkable stability based on the alliance between the Ba'th Party, the military, and the bureaucracy, which was led by the shrewd and tenacious President Assad and supported by a predominantly 'Alawite network of officials and officers, many of whom repressed their opponents by harsh methods. The opponents of the Ba'th-military-'Alawite system were found especially among the Sunni majority of the population, in the cities outside Damascus, and inside merchant groups. Government troops in 1982 suppressed an uprising of the outlawed Muslim Brotherhood in the city of Ḥamāh. The conflict left the city centre destroyed and thousands dead (estimates of civilian casualties range from 5,000 to 10,000).

Ideology and Foreign Policy to 1990

Under Ba'th rule the country's foreign policy was driven by the Arab-Israeli conflict, which resulted in a number of Syrian military defeats. In the June War (1967), the Golan Heights of Syria came under Israeli occupation, and in the October (Yom Kippur) War (1973), in spite of initial successes, Syria lost even more territory. Syria's Pan-Arab credentials and its alliance with the Soviet Union were strained by Syria's support of non-Arab Iran against Iraq—motivated in part by the long-standing rivalry between the Iraqi and Syrian Ba'thists, competing goals for regional dominance, and personal animosity between Assad and Iraqi president Ṣaddām Ḥussein—during the Iran-Iraq War (1980–88).

Syrian involvement in Lebanon also influenced its foreign policy. In 1976 Syria intervened militarily in the Lebanese civil war, leading to a brief but damaging clash with Israel in 1982. After 1985 Assad slowly reestablished limited Syrian control in Lebanon. Following the end of the Lebanese civil war in 1990, Syria and Lebanon signed a series of treaties that granted special privileges to Syria by establishing joint institutions in the fields of defense, foreign policy, and economic matters.

Arab nationalism also played a major role in Syrian culture under the Ba'thists. Novels, poems, short stories, plays, and paintings often emphasized historical themes, the Palestinian problem, Socialist Realism, folk art, and opposition to foreign imperialism. The Ba'thist governments tried to bring these ideas to both the countryside and the cities through building cultural centres, sponsoring films, and promoting television and radio.

In spite of growing revenues from oil exports and increased irrigation resulting from the Euphrates Dam, Syria's economy began to stagnate in the 1980s. Rapid population increase hindered economic growth, while the intensification of agriculture ran into natural barriers, such as the limited availability of fresh water and the high cost of desalination. Industrial development was slowed by bottlenecks in production. Inflation, government corruption, smuggling, foreign debts, a stifling bureaucracy, and scant success in encouraging private sector investments also posed severe economic problems, as did spending on the military and on the intervention in Lebanon. Assad hoped to overcome some of these economic difficulties by obtaining aid from the rich oil states of the Middle East. As the Soviet Union disintegrated, Syria turned to China for military supplies.

Bashar al-Assad

(b. September 11, 1965, Damascus, Syria)

Bashar al-Assad became the president of Syria in 2000. He succeeded his father, Ḥafiz al-Assad, who had ruled Syria since 1971.

Assad studied medicine at the University of Damascus and graduated as a general practitioner in 1988. He then trained to become an ophthalmologist at a Damascus military hospital and in 1992 moved to London to continue his studies. In 1994 his older brother, Basil, who had been designated his father's heir apparent, was killed in an automobile accident, and Bashar returned to Syria to take his brother's place. He trained at a military academy and eventually gained the rank of colonel in the elite Presidential Guard. On June 18, 2000, after the death of his father on June 10, Assad was appointed secretary-general of the ruling Ba'th Party, and two days later the party congress nominated him as its candidate for the presidency. The national legislature approved the nomination, and on July 10, running unopposed, Assad was elected to a seven-year term.

As president, Assad announced that he would not support policies that might threaten the dominance of the Ba'th Party, but he slightly loosened government restrictions on freedom of expression and the press. He also emphasized the need to modernize the country's economy, which had been mostly government-controlled and was heavily dependent on oil exports. In early 2005, after the assassination of Lebanon's former prime minister Rafiq al-Hariri, Assad—under pressure from Western and Arab nations—committed to the removal of Syrian troops and intelligence services from Lebanon, where Syrian forces had been stationed since a 1976 military intervention. Although a UN investigation appeared to indicate some level of Syrian participation in the assassination of Hariri, the involvement of the Assad administration was not conclusively determined in 2006, and the investigation continued.

Though reform hopes for Assad's first term had been met mainly with cosmetic changes, minor progress had been made with economic reforms. In 2007 Assad was reelected by a nearly unanimous majority to a second term as president through elections generally received by critics and opponents as a sham.

Foreign Engagement and Domestic Change Since 1990

Foreign Policy

Syria condemned the Iraqi invasion and annexation of Kuwait in August 1990. More than 20,000 Syrian troops joined the UN-authorized coalition in Saudi Arabia, and Syrian forces helped liberate Kuwait from Iraq during the brief 1991 war.

Syria participated in Arab-Israeli peace talks starting with the Madrid conference in October and November 1991 and intermittently engaged in direct negotiations with Israel throughout the 1990s over the return of the occupied Golan Heights and a possible peace accord between the two countries. Although the negotiations periodically showed promise, the climate of the discussion fluctuated considerably, and by the end of the decade, the dialogue between the two sides had garnered little success.

Relations between Syria and Iraq unexpectedly warmed somewhat, particularly following Assad's death in 2000. This sudden thaw was also attributed in part to Syria's insecurity over deteriorating relations with neighbouring Turkey, with whom Syria had engaged in numerous disputes over water rights and whose growing ties with Israel were seen as a threat. By 1998 ongoing Turkish accusations of Syrian support for the militant Kurdish nationalist Kurdistan Workers' Party (PKK) had further destabilized Syrian-Turkish relations. Following an agreement reached between the two countries late that year, Syria forced PKK leader Abdullah Öcalan from the country and agreed upon the closure of PKK camps within Syria.

In addition to a series of agreements of partnership and cooperation with Lebanon following the end of that country's civil war, Syria maintained a sizable contingent of armed forces on Lebanese soil. In the years that followed, however, Syria's ongoing presence in Lebanon grew increasingly untenable, particularly in the wake of the 2005 assassination of Lebanon's former prime minister Rafiq al-Hariri, who had fallen out with his country's pro-Syrian administration. International relations became strained amid popular Lebanese protests against Syria's presence and widespread suspicions of Syrian involvement in Hariri's death. Sharp international pressure was applied to the country to pull out of Lebanon, and by mid-2005 Syrian forces had withdrawn. The following year, suspicions persisted that the Assad administration had been directly involved in the Hariri assassination, a claim that was supported—though not confirmed—in 2006 by the initial findings of an ongoing UN investigation.

Domestic Challenges

Because of the country's earlier instability and record of military coups, throughout the 1990s the question of who would eventually succeed President Assad was a principal domestic concern. The prominent public posture assumed by Basil al-Assad, the president's eldest son, appeared to indicate his emergence as successor. Following Basil's death in an automobile accident in 1994, however, Assad increasingly groomed his younger son, Bashar al-Assad, who had been studying in London, to govern after him. Following Assad's death in 2000, Bashar succeeded his father in the presidency.

With his election in 2000, high hopes lay with the younger Assad: citizens and international observers looked to the new president to maintain a degree of order and continuity, provide a level of political openness acceptable to the Syrian people, and carry on the campaign begun under his father of implementing government reform and rooting out deeply entrenched corruption. A historic visit by Pope John Paul II, improving relations with Iraq, and Assad's release of 600 political prisoners early in his term signaled the potential for significant change. Those seeking liberalization were soon bitterly disappointed, however. While some changes, such as economic-related measures, slowly showed progress, many other reforms failed to materialize. The 2001 detention of pro-reform activists and the dwindling period of tentative reform that had marked the brief political opening known as the Damascus Spring cut these hopes short. In 2007, amid an opposition boycott, Assad secured his second term in office. Critics denounced the elections, in which Assad ran unopposed and achieved just under 100 percent of votes cast, as a sham. At the start of Assad's second term, Syria's capacity for meaningful political change remained yet to be seen.

Chapter 6

Lebanon: The Land and Its People

Lebanon is a mountainous country located on the eastern shore of the Mediterranean Sea. Consisting of a narrow strip of coastal territory, Lebanon is one of the world's smaller sovereign states. Lebanon is bounded to the north and east by Syria, to the south by Israel, and to the west by the Mediterranean Sea.

Lebanon has a heterogeneous society composed of numerous ethnic, religious, and kinship groups. Long-standing attachments and local communalism antedate the creation of the present territorial and political entity and continue to survive with remarkable tenacity.

Lebanon's geography, with mountains as well as plains, is varied and complex, and it boasts a diverse population as well.

Ethnically, the Lebanese population is a complex admixture among which Phoenician, Greek, Armenian, and Arab elements can be detected. Minorities residing in the country include Kurds and Armenians.

RELIEF

As in any mountainous region, the physical geography of Lebanon is extremely complex and varied. Landforms, climate, soils, and vegetation undergo some sharp and striking changes within short distances. Four distinct physiographic regions may be distinguished: a narrow coastal plain along the Mediterranean Sea, the Lebanon Mountains, Bekaa Valley, and the Anti-Lebanon and Hermon ranges running parallel to the Lebanese Mountains.

The coastal plain is narrow and discontinuous, almost disappearing in places. It is formed of river-deposited alluvium and marine sediments, which alternate suddenly with rocky beaches and sandy bays, and is generally fertile. In the far north it expands to form the ʿAkkār Plain.

The snowcapped Lebanon Mountains are one of the most prominent features of the country's landscape. The range, rising steeply from the coast, forms a ridge of limestone and sandstone, cut by narrow and deep gorges. It runs parallel to the Mediterranean for much of the country's length and varies in width from 6 to 35 miles (10 to 56 km). Its maximum elevation is at Qurnat al-Sawdāʾ (10,131 feet [3,088 m]) in the north, where the renowned cedars of Lebanon grow in the shadow of the peak. The range then gradually slopes to the south, rising again to a second peak, Jabal Ṣannīn (8,842 feet [2,695 m]), northeast of Beirut. To the south the range branches westward to form the Shūf Mountains and at

Lebanon Mountains

The Lebanon Mountains (Arabic: Jabal Lubnān; French: Mont Liban) extend almost the entire length of Lebanon, paralleling the Mediterranean coast for about 150 miles (240 km), with northern outliers extending into Syria.

The northern section, north of the saddle, or pass, of Ḍahr al-Baydar (through which the Beirut–Damascus railroad and highway run), is the widest and loftiest part of the mountains, which average 7,000 feet (2,100 m) above sea level, with a few snowcapped peaks, including Qurnat al-Sawdā', at 10,131 feet (3,088 m). On the western flanks, east of Bsharrī, are the remaining groves of the renowned cedars of Lebanon. South of the pass the mountains average elevations of 5,000–6,000 feet (1,500–1,800 m). In southern Lebanon they are broken by the 900-foot-deep (275 m) gorge of the Līṭānī River (Nahr Al-Līṭānī). Although the porous limestone of the mountains forms poor, thin soil, it has helped create numerous underground springs that make irrigated cultivation of the lower and middle slopes possible. A variety of tree crops (including olives, apricots, and apples) are grown on the coastal side. The view presented by the snow-clad peaks may have given Lebanon its name in antiquity. *Laban* is Aramaic for "white."

its southern reaches gives way to the hills of Galilee, which are lower.

The Bekaa Valley lies between the Lebanon Mountains in the west and the Anti-Lebanon Mountains in the east. Its fertile soils consist of alluvial deposits from the mountains on either side. The valley, approximately 110 miles (180 km) long and from 6 to 16 miles (10 to 26 km) wide, is part of the great East African Rift System. In the south the Bekaa Valley becomes hilly and rugged, blending into the foothills of Mount Hermon to form the upper Jordan Valley.

Līṭānī River

The Līṭānī River (Arabic: Nahr Al-Līṭānī; Latin: Leontes) is the chief river of Lebanon, rising in a low divide west of Baalbek and flowing southwestward through the Bekaa Valley between the Lebanon and Anti-Lebanon mountains. Near Marj 'Uyūn it bends sharply west and cuts a spectacular gorge up to 900 feet (275 metres) deep through the Lebanon Mountains to the Mediterranean south of Sidon. The river's lower course is known as Qāsimiyyah. Although the river's total length is only about 90 miles (145 km), its waters irrigate one of Lebanon's most extensive farming regions, the Bekaa Valley. The Litani River Authority, established in 1954, was to have provided for an increase in irrigated land, generation of electricity, and development of recreational areas; however, the main achievement of the project was later limited to the establishment of electrical power plants.

The Anti-Lebanon range starts with a high peak in the north. It then slopes southward until it is interrupted by Mount Hermon (9,232 feet [2,814 m]).

DRAINAGE

Lebanese rivers, though numerous, are mostly winter torrents, draining the western slopes of the Lebanon Mountains. The only exception is the Līṭānī River (90 miles [145 km] long), which rises near the famed ruins of Baalbek (Ba'labakk) and flows southward in the Bekaa Valley to empty into the Mediterranean near historic Tyre. The two other important rivers are the Orontes, which rises north of the Bekaa Valley and flows northward, and the Kabīr.

SOILS

Soil quality and makeup in Lebanon vary by region. The shallow limestone soil of the mountains provides a relatively poor topsoil. The lower and middle slopes, however, are intensively cultivated, the terraced hills standing as a scenic relic of the ingenious tillers of the past. On the coast and in the northern mountains, reddish topsoils with a high clay content retain moisture and provide fertile land for agriculture, although they are subject to considerable erosion.

CLIMATE

There are sharp local contrasts in the country's climatic conditions. Lebanon is included in the Mediterranean climatic region, which extends westward to the Atlantic Ocean. Winter storms formed over the ocean move eastward through the Mediterranean, bringing precipitation. In summer, however, the Mediterranean receives little or no precipitation. The climate of Lebanon is generally subtropical and is characterized by hot, dry summers and mild, humid winters. Mean daily maximum temperatures range from the low 90s °F (low 30s °C) in July to the low 60s °F (mid-10s °C) on the coast and low 50s °F (low 10s °C) in the Bekaa Valley in January. Mean minimum temperatures in January are in the low 50s °F on the coast and the mid-30s °F (about 2 °C) in the Bekaa Valley. At 5,000 feet (1,524 metres), the elevation of the highest settlements, these are reduced by about 15 °F (8 °C).

Nearly all precipitation falls in winter, averaging 30 to 40 inches (750 to 1,000 mm) on the coast and rising to more than 50 inches (1,270 mm) in higher elevations. The Bekaa Valley is drier and receives 15 to 25 inches (380 to

640 mm). On the higher mountaintops, this precipitation falls as heavy snow that remains until early summer.

PLANT AND ANIMAL LIFE

Lebanon was heavily forested in ancient and medieval times, and its timber—particularly its famed cedar—was exported for building and shipbuilding. The natural vegetation, however, has been grazed, burned, and cut for so long that little of it is regenerated. What survives is a wild Mediterranean vegetation of brush and low trees, mostly oaks, pines, cypresses, firs, junipers, and carobs.

Few large wild animals survive in Lebanon, though bears are occasionally seen in the mountains. Among the smaller animals, deer, wildcats, hedgehogs, squirrels, martens,

*Cedar of Lebanon (*Cedrus libani*).* G. E. Hyde—Natural History Photographic Agency/EB Inc.

dormice, and hares are found. Numerous migratory birds from Africa and Europe visit Lebanon. Flamingos, pelicans, cormorants, ducks, herons, and snipes frequent the marshes; eagles, buzzards, kites, falcons, and hawks inhabit the mountains; and owls, kingfishers, cuckoos, and woodpeckers are common.

Although Lebanon's diverse and abundant plant and animal life suffered a heavy toll during the country's lengthy civil war and subsequent conflicts, the post–civil war period was marked by the rise of fledgling environmental groups and movements that worked toward the creation of protected areas and parks in Lebanon's sensitive ecological areas.

ETHNIC AND LINGUISTIC GROUPS

Ethnically, the Lebanese compose a mixture in which Phoenician, Greek, Armenian, and Arab elements are discernible. Within the larger Lebanese community, ethnic minorities including Armenian and Kurdish populations are also present. Arabic is the official language, although smaller proportions of the population are Armenian- or Kurdish-speaking; French and English are also spoken. Syriac is used in some of the churches of the Maronites (Roman Catholics following an Eastern rite).

RELIGION

Perhaps the most distinctive feature of Lebanon's social structure is its varied religious composition. Since the 7th century Lebanon has served as a refuge for persecuted Christian and Muslim sects. As religion and government in Lebanon are deeply and formally intertwined, the relative proportions of the country's religious communities are a highly sensitive matter. There has not been an

Druze

The Druze are members of a relatively small Middle Eastern religious sect characterized by an eclectic system of doctrines as well as a cohesion and loyalty among its members. At times politically significant, such cohesion has enabled them to maintain their close-knit identity and distinctive faith through almost a thousand years of turbulent history. They numbered more than 250,000 in the late 20th century and lived mostly in Lebanon, with smaller communities in Israel and Syria. They call themselves *muwaḥḥidūn* ("monotheists").

The Druze permit no intermarriage, and conversion has been prohibited since 1043. In these circumstances the survival of their religion and community across almost a millennium is the more remarkable in that their religious system is kept secret not only from the outside world but in part even from their own number. Only an elite of initiates, known as *ʿuqqāl* ("knowers"), participate fully in their religious services and have access to the secret teachings of the *ḥikmah*, the Druze religious doctrine. A Druze is allowed to deny his or her faith outwardly if his or her life is in danger. This concession, or *taqiyyah,* is allowed according to *Al-Taʿlīm* ("Instruction"), the anonymously written "catechism" of Druze faith.

official census since 1932, however, and the data depicting Lebanon's confessional composition are variable. In general terms, Muslims are the most numerous group overall. Among the three Muslim denominations, the Shīʿites and the Sunnis are the largest, and the Druze constitute a small percentage. Among Lebanon's Christian population, the Maronites, which form the largest of the Catholic groups, are the largest Christian community overall. The Greek Orthodox community, the largest of the Orthodox groups, is the second largest Christian group overall. There is also a very small Jewish minority.

SETTLEMENT PATTERNS

Most of the population lives on the coastal plain, and progressively fewer people are found farther inland. Rural villages are sited according to water supply and the availability of land, frequently including terraced agriculture in the mountains. Northern villages are relatively prosperous and have some modern architecture. Villages in the south have been generally poorer and less stable: local agricultural land is less fertile, and, because of their proximity to Israel, many villages have been subject to frequent dislocation, invasion, and destruction since 1975. Most cities are located on the coast. They have been inundated by migrants and displaced persons, and numerous, often poor, suburbs have been created as a result. Before 1975 many villages and cities were composed of several different religious groups, usually living together in harmony, and rural architecture reflected a unity of style irrespective of religious identity. Since the civil war began, a realignment has moved thousands of Christians north of Beirut along the coast and thousands of Muslims south or east of Beirut. Thus, settlement patterns reflect the chasms separating sections of the Lebanese people from each other.

DEMOGRAPHIC TRENDS

Lebanon's birth rate is slightly below the world's average, while its death rate is well below the global average. More than one-fourth of the population is younger than age 15, with more than one-half younger than age 30. Life expectancy in Lebanon is higher than the world average. One of the most salient demographic features of Lebanon is the uneven distribution of its population. The country's overall density varies regionally and is on the whole much lower than that of Beirut and the surrounding area but much higher than that of the most sparsely populated Bekaa Valley.

Before the civil war began, the movement of people from rural areas was a major factor in the country's soaring rate of urbanization. Most of the internal migration was to Beirut, which accounted for the great majority of Lebanon's urban population. The civil war led to a substantial return of people to their villages and to a large migration abroad, primarily to the United States, Europe, Latin America, Australia, and parts of the Middle East. Within Lebanon, it also led to a process of population dispersal and exchange in many areas that had previously been characterized by the coexistence of Christians and Muslims, and postwar efforts to reverse this process through programs meant to resettle the displaced were not immediately successful. Following the warfare between Hezbollah (Lebanese Shīʿite militia group and political party) and Israeli armed forces in 2006, many more Lebanese citizens—an estimated one million residents, particularly those living in the country's south—were displaced from their homes.

CHAPTER 7

The Lebanese Economy

In the years before the outbreak of civil war, Lebanon enjoyed status as a regional and commercial centre. The Lebanese economy was characterized by a minimum of government intervention in private enterprise combined with an income– and profit–tax-free environment. Although imports far outstripped exports, elements such as tourism and remittances from labourers working abroad helped balance the trade deficit. Income was generally on the rise, and Lebanese products were finding a place on the international market.

For the first 10 years of the civil war, the Lebanese economy proved remarkably resilient. After the mid-1980s, however, the value of the Lebanese pound plummeted as the continued destruction of the country's infrastructure took its toll. After the civil war, Lebanon embarked on an ambitious program of social and economic reconstruction that entailed extensive renovation of the country's flagging infrastructure. Initiated by Prime Minister Rafiq al-Hariri in the 1990s, it aimed to revive Beirut as a regional financial and commercial centre. Beirut's reconstruction program made considerable progress in the late 20th and early 21st centuries, albeit at the expense of an increasing internal and external governmental debt load: much of the rebuilding program was financed through internal borrowing, which led to the emergence of both budget deficits and a growing public debt. Yet, to attract and encourage investment, tax rates were reduced. This led to severe budgetary austerity, resulting in only limited investment in Lebanon's social infrastructure and a growing reliance on regressive indirect taxation to meet budgetary shortfalls. Hence, while a fraction of Lebanese became very rich in post-war Lebanon, at the beginning of the 21st century some one-third of the Lebanese population lived below the poverty line.

AGRICULTURE

Arable land is scarce, but the climate and the relatively abundant water supply from springs favour the intensive cultivation of a variety of crops on mountain slopes and in the coastal region. On the irrigated coastal plain, market vegetables, bananas, and citrus crops are grown. In the foothills the principal crops are olives, grapes, tobacco, figs, and almonds. At higher elevations (about 1,500 feet [460 m]), peaches, apricots, plums, and cherries are planted, while apples and pears thrive at an elevation of about 3,000 feet (900 m). Sugar beets, cereals, and vegetables are the main crops cultivated in Al-Biqāʿ. Poultry is a major source of agricultural income, and goats, sheep, and cattle are also raised.

As a result of the continued violence, many small farmers have lost their livestock, and there has been a noticeable decrease in the production of many agricultural crops. The production of hemp, the source of hashish, has flourished in the Bekaa Valley, however, and the hashish is exported illegally through ports along the coast.

RESOURCES AND POWER

The mineral resources of Lebanon are few. There are deposits of high-grade iron ore and lignite; building-stone quarries; high-quality sand, suitable for glass manufacture; and lime. The Līṭānī River hydroelectric project generates electricity and has increased the amount of irrigated land

With a scarcity of available land for harvesting, olives are one crop that makes good use of the foothills. Joseph Barrak/AFP/Getty Images

for agriculture. Lebanon's power networks and facilities were damaged during the country's civil war and by Israeli air strikes carried out during the periodic warfare of the late 20th and early 21st centuries.

MANUFACTURING

Leading industries in Lebanon include the manufacture of food products; cement, bricks, and ceramics; wood and wood products; and textiles. Many of the country's industries were harmed by the civil war, and its effects on the textile industry were especially severe. Although some of the country's large complexes were unharmed, Beirut's industrial belt was razed. In addition, Israel's occupation of the Lebanese south led to an influx of Israeli goods that also harmed Lebanese industries. The construction industry initially played a significant role in the postwar reconstruction that began in the early 1990s. Recurrent violence in the late 20th and early 21st centuries, however, caused further damage to Lebanese industry and infrastructure.

FINANCE

During the first 10 years of the civil war, the finance sector of Lebanon's economy, including banking and insurance, showed an impressive expansion, and the monetary reserves of Lebanon continued to rise in spite of political uncertainties. The strength of the Lebanese pound and of the balance-of-payments position reflected large inflows of capital, mostly from Lebanese living abroad (whose numbers rose considerably during and after the civil war) and from the high level of liquidity of commercial banks. By 1983, however, inflows from Lebanese living abroad had

Bekaa Valley

The Bekaa Valley (also spelled Beqaa; Arabic: Al-Biqāʿ) is a broad valley of central Lebanon, extending in a northeast-southwest direction for 75 miles (120 km) along the Līṭānī and Orontes rivers, between the Lebanon Mountains to the west and Anti-Lebanon Mountains to the east. The valley contains nearly half of Lebanon's arable land but is not as intensively farmed as the country's coastal plain because of less precipitation and a wider variation in temperature. Crops grown in this mostly dry-farmed area are grains, with fruits and vegetables of secondary importance. Main towns include Zaḥlah, noted for its vineyards and for its production of arrack (an alcoholic beverage made from dates); Baalbek, the site of several outstanding Roman ruins; and Rīyāq. In the late 20th century, the Bekaa Valley was the scene of continued skirmishes between the Syrian and certain Lebanese and Palestine Liberation Organization (PLO) forces and Israel.

begun to decrease, and the value of the Lebanese pound fell dramatically.

As a result, two major challenges for post–civil war Lebanon were to secure enough capital to finance its reconstruction program and to reestablish the value of the Lebanese pound through a program of economic stabilization. Lebanon was forced to rely on capital-bond issues in the European market as well as domestic borrowing through the issue of treasury bills, which resulted in a rise in the level of both domestic and international indebtedness. In spite of some gains in the early 21st century, the economy suffered marked declines with both the assassination of former prime minister Hariri in 2005 and the destruction wrought by the 2006 warfare between Israel and Hezbollah.

TRADE

Beirut's seaport and airport and the country's free economic and foreign-exchange systems, favourable interest rates, and banking secrecy law (modeled upon that of Switzerland) all contributed to Lebanon's preeminence of trade and services, particularly before the outset of the country's civil war.

During the civil war, however, widespread smuggling, covert foreign aid to armed groups, and illegal drug production combined to disguise the country's pattern of trade. Exports—chiefly precious metal jewelry and stones, electrical equipment, base and fabricated metals, and chemical products—are sent mainly to Middle Eastern countries. Imports such as mineral products (i.e., petroleum), food and live animals, and transport and electrical equipment come mostly from the United States, China, and western Europe. A huge trade deficit has been partly covered by "invisible" items such as foreign remittances and government loans. A series of economic and trade agreements signed with Syria after the end of the civil war resulted in a considerable degree of economic and commercial integration between the two countries.

SERVICES

Before the civil war, the growth of the service sector—which generated the overwhelming proportion of national income and employed the largest proportion of the labour force—was related mainly to international transport and trade and to the position of Beirut as a centre of international banking and tourism. The abundance of natural scenery, historic sites, hotels, bars, nightclubs, restaurants, seaside and mountain resorts, outdoor sports facilities, and international cultural festivals in Lebanon traditionally helped maintain tourism as one of the country's most important year-round industries.

Although all economic sectors were affected by the warfare, the detriment to the service sector was among the most profound. Following the end of the civil war in 1990, extensive reconstruction programs aimed to return Beirut to its status as a hub of finance and tourism, although progress was disrupted by periods of ongoing violence in the late 20th and early 21st centuries.

LABOUR AND TAXATION

Large-scale unemployment and the emigration of many skilled labourers during the Lebanese civil war had a devastating effect on the country's workforce. As a result, numerous sectors were greatly hindered during the civil war period, with industry, construction, and transport and communications suffering the most significant contractions in workforce populations.

Lebanon has a comparatively well-developed labour movement. Although faced with significant challenges, including government interference and restrictions, trade unions have secured some tangible gains, such as fringe benefits, collective bargaining contracts, and better working conditions. During the civil war, divisions in many of the trade unions weakened their normal functions, and many of their members joined the warring factions. Many others emigrated. The end of the civil war saw the revival of Lebanon's trade union movement, which became an active participant in Lebanon's postwar civil society and demonstrated against the rising cost of living in the country and the increase in indirect taxes on such items as gasoline and oil. Lebanon's trade unions are organized into confederations, including the General Confederation of Lebanese Workers (Confédération Générale des Travailleurs au Liban).

A minimum wage is set by the Labour Code, and legislation provides for cost-of-living increases, such as those that occurred prior to, during, and after the civil war, mainly because of a substantial rise in the cost of housing, education, food, and petroleum products. Tax revenues are an important source of income for the Lebanese government, among which domestic taxes on goods and services and income tax are the most significant.

TRANSPORTATION

As in antiquity, Lebanon's location makes it a vital crossroads between East and West. The road network traversing Lebanon includes international highways, which form part of major land routes connecting Europe with the Arab countries and the East. There are also national highways, paved secondary roads, and unpaved roads.

Numerous ports lie along the seacoast. Berths for oil tankers have been built offshore at Tripoli and at Al-Zahrānī, near Sidon, where pipeline terminals and refineries also are located. The principal cargo and passenger port is that of Beirut, which has a free zone and storage facilities for transit shipments. The port has been expanded and deepened, and a large storage silo (for wheat and other grains) has been built, but port facilities were severely damaged during the civil war and the postwar fighting. The harbour at Jūniyah has grown in importance.

Beirut International Airport was one of the busiest airports in the Middle East before the civil war. Its runways were built to handle the largest jet airplanes in service, and a number of international airlines used Beirut regularly. After 1990, renovations to Beirut's airport were undertaken to facilitate a return to its prewar importance.

At the end of the civil war, Lebanon's transportation infrastructure on the whole required significant reconstruction. Many roads were rebuilt, including a highway along the coast from Tripoli to Sidon. Although some repairs were undertaken in 2004, Lebanon's railway system—which included lines along the coast and up the Bekaa Valley, as well as a cog railway across the Lebanon Mountains—remained out of service in the years following the civil war. Many transport facilities—including the airport, ports, and major highways—were damaged anew during the warfare between Israel and Hezbollah in mid-2006.

CHAPTER 8

Lebanese Government and Society

Modern Lebanon is a unitary multiparty republic with a parliamentary system of government. Its constitution, promulgated in 1926 during the French mandate and modified by several subsequent amendments, provides for a unicameral Chamber of Deputies (renamed the National Assembly in 1979) elected for a term of four years by universal adult suffrage (women attained the right to vote and eligibility to run for office in 1953). According to the 1989 Ṭā'if Accord, parliamentary seats are apportioned equally between Christian and Muslim sects, thereby replacing an earlier ratio that had favoured Christians. This sectarian distribution is also to be observed in appointments to public office. This confessional system is prone to political deadlock, however, such as that in late 2007, when a boycott by one faction prevented the National Assembly from reaching a quorum on the replacement of the outgoing president. As a result, the post lay unoccupied for months.

The head of state is the president, who is elected by a two-thirds majority of the National Assembly for a term of six years and is eligible to serve consecutive terms. By an unwritten convention the president must be a Maronite Christian, the premier a Sunni Muslim, and the speaker of the National Assembly a Shīʿite. The president, in consultation with the speaker of the National Assembly and the parliamentary deputies, invites a Sunni Muslim to form a cabinet, and the cabinet members' portfolios are organized to reflect the sectarian balance. The cabinet, which holds more executive power than the president, requires a vote of confidence from the assembly in order to remain in power. A vote of no confidence, however, is rarely exercised in practice. A cabinet usually falls because of internal dissension, societal strife, or pressure exerted by foreign states.

LOCAL GOVERNMENT

Lebanon is divided into *muḥāfaẓāt* (governorates) administered by the *muḥāfiẓ* (governor), who represents the central government. The governorates are further divided into *aqḍiyyah* (districts), each of which is presided over by a *qā'im-maqām* (district chief), who, along with the governor, supervises local government. Municipalities (communities with at least 500 inhabitants) elect their own councils, which in turn elect mayors and vice-mayors. Villages and towns (more than 50 and fewer than 500 inhabitants) elect a *mukhtār* (headman) and a council of elders, who serve on an honorary basis. Officers of local governments serve four-year terms.

JUSTICE

The system of law and justice is mostly modeled on French concepts. The judiciary consists of courts of the first instance, courts of appeal, courts of cassation, and a Court of Justice that handles cases affecting state security. The Council of State is a court that deals with administrative affairs. In addition, there are religious courts that deal with matters of personal status (such as inheritance, marriage, and property matters) as they pertain to autonomous communities. Stipulations in the Ṭā'if Accord have led to the post–civil war establishment of a Constitutional Council, which is empowered to monitor the constitutionality of laws and handle disputes in the electoral process. In spite of the country's well-developed legal system and a very high proportion of lawyers, significant numbers of disputes and personal grievances are resolved outside the courts. Justice by feud and vendetta continues.

POLITICAL PROCESS

The political system in Lebanon remains a blend of secular and traditional features. Until 1975 the country appeared to support liberal and democratic institutions, yet in effect it had hardly any of the political instruments of a civil polity. Its political parties, parliamentary blocs, and pressure groups were so closely identified with parochial, communal, and personal loyalties that they often failed to serve the larger national purpose of the society. The National Pact of 1943, a sort of Christian-Muslim entente, sustained the national entity (*al-kiyān*), yet this sense of identity was neither national nor civic. The agreement reached at Ṭā'if essentially secured a return to the same political process and its mixture of formal and informal political logic.

Provisions are in place for power sharing among Lebanon's various sectarian groups. Women have not typically participated in the government. The first position in the cabinet to be held by a woman occurred in 2005. Palestinian refugees in Lebanon do not enjoy political rights and do not participate in the government.

SECURITY

The armed forces consist of an army, an air force, and a navy. Lebanon also has a paramilitary gendarmerie and a police force. During the civil war the army practically disintegrated when splinter groups joined the different warring factions. Reconstruction of the Lebanese armed forces has been attempted, particularly with the assistance first of the United States and then of Syria, with substantial effect. Responsibility for maintaining security and order has often fallen to the various political and religious factions and to foreign occupiers.

HEALTH AND WELFARE

Public health services are largely concentrated in the cities, although the government increasingly directs medical aid into rural areas. As in the field of social welfare, nongovernmental voluntary associations—mostly religious, communal, or ethnic—are active. The Lebanese diet is generally satisfactory, and the high standard of living and the favourable climate have served to reduce the incidence of many diseases that are still common in other Middle Eastern countries.

Lebanon has a large number of skilled medical personnel, and hospital facilities are adequate under normal circumstances. Following the destruction of the civil war, considerable efforts—largely on the part of Lebanon's religious communities and nonprofit sector—were made to upgrade the infrastructure and services in the health and social welfare sectors.

The National Social Security Fund, which is not fully implemented, provides sickness and maternity insurance, labour-accident and occupational-disease insurance, family benefits, and termination-of-service benefits.

HOUSING

In response to the need for low-cost housing, the Popular Housing Law was enacted in the 1960s, providing for the rehabilitation of substandard housing. Prior to the civil war a substantial percentage of homes were without bathrooms, and thousands of families, including Palestinian refugees, were living in improvised accommodations. When an economic boom attracted villagers to the capital, the housing shortage worsened considerably. The civil war drastically increased the problem. Thousands of homes in battle zones were destroyed, and entire villages were evacuated and others occupied. The result was chaos in which property rights were violated as a matter of course. The government, in an attempt to remedy the situation, set up a Housing Bank to make housing loans.

EDUCATION

Lebanon's well-developed system of education reaches all levels of the population, and literacy rates are among the highest in the Middle East. Although education was once almost exclusively the responsibility of religious communities or foreign groups, public schools have sprung up across the country. Nevertheless, the majority of Lebanese students continue to be educated at private schools, which are generally considered more favourably than their public counterparts. Although more than two-fifths of students were enrolled in public schools in the early 1970s, at the end of the civil war the number had dropped to about one-third.

The five-year primary school program is followed either by a seven-year secondary program (leading to the official baccalaureate certificate) or by a four-year program of technical or vocational training. Major universities include the American University of Beirut (1866), the Université Saint-Joseph (1875; subsidized by the French government and administered by the Jesuit order), the Lebanese University (Université Libanaise; 1951), and the Beirut Arab University (1960; an affiliate of the University of Alexandria).

SOCIAL AND ECONOMIC DIVISION

Lebanese society was able for a long time to give a semblance of relative economic stability. The existence of a large middle-income group, in addition to the political and

At the American University of Beirut students can attend schools of medicine, pharmacy, and nursing. Joseph Barrak/AFP/Getty Images

American University of Beirut

The American University of Beirut is a private, nondenominational, coeducational international and intercultural university in Beirut, chartered in 1863 by the state of New York, U.S., as the Syrian Protestant College. Classes started in 1866. Although founded by the American Protestant Mission to Lebanon, the school was set up as an autonomous organization and has no official relationship with any religious body. Its present name was adopted in 1920. The educational philosophy is similar to that of an American university, but its program is adapted to the educational needs of the Middle East. Some 80 percent of its students come from the Arab countries of the Middle East and North Africa. A school of medicine was opened in 1867, a school of pharmacy in 1871, and a school of nursing and a hospital in 1905. All are important to the country, and the hospital was the main medical centre of Beirut in the early years of the Lebanese Civil War (1975–90). The university managed to remain in operation during the war, but most of the non-Arab members of its faculty had fled Lebanon by the late 1980s.

social legitimacy of kinship ties and religious and communal attachments, reinforced the veneer that masked the growing socioeconomic dislocations. The interaction of these factors covered up the growing class polarization, especially around the industrial belt that encircled Beirut. The eruption of civil conflict in 1975, and the state of chaos that ensued, is attributable in part to the fact that the system of government was unresponsive to the acute social problems and grievances.

The problems of increasing socioeconomic disparity and government inaction continued into Lebanon's post–civil war period. In spite of the visible success of some aspects of Lebanon's reconstruction program, the reality of the country's postwar economic situation has been characterized by a dwindling middle class and the descent of many Lebanese citizens into poverty.

Lebanese Cultural Life

Historically, Lebanon is heir to a long succession of Mediterranean cultures—Phoenician, Greek, and Arab. Its cultural milieu continues to show clear manifestations of a rich and diverse heritage. As an Arab country, Lebanon shares more than a common language with neighbouring Arab states, with a similar cultural heritage and common interests.

Many of Lebanon's rich cultural sites have been designated UNESCO World Heritage sites: the remains of the city of 'Anjar (founded by al-Walīd in the early 8th century); the ruins of successive cultures at the old Phoenician cities of Baalbek, Byblos, and Tyre; and the Christian monasteries in Wadi Qādīshā, together with the nearby remains of a sacred forest of long-prized cedar.

DAILY LIFE AND SOCIAL CUSTOMS

Lebanon's diverse culture is a result of its admixture of various religious, linguistic, and socioeconomic groups.

Ruins at 'Anjar, Lebanon. Photos.com/Jupiterimages

CHAPTER 9

Family and kinship play a central role in Lebanese social relationships, in both the private and public spheres. Although family structure is traditionally largely patriarchal, women are active in education and politics.

Because of the country's diverse religious makeup, Lebanese citizens observe a variety of holidays. Those celebrated by the Christian community include Easter and Christmas, the dates of which vary, as elsewhere, between the Catholic and Orthodox communities. 'Īd al-Fiṭr (which marks the end of Ramadan), 'Īd al-Aḍḥā (which marks the culmination of the hajj), and the Prophet Muhammad's birthday are celebrated by Lebanese Muslims. 'Āshūrā', a holiday particular to Shī'ite Muslims, is also observed. In addition, Martyrs' Day is observed on May 6 and Independence Day on November 22.

THE ARTS

Lebanon's antiquities and ruins have provided not only inspiration for artists but also magnificent backdrops for annual music festivals, most notably the Baalbek International Festival. At one time, international opera, ballet, symphony, and drama companies of nearly all nationalities competed to enrich the cultural life of Beirut. Following the end of the civil war in 1990, Lebanon's cultural life gradually began to reemerge, though that revival remained subject to interruption by periods of violence in the late 20th and early 21st centuries.

Lebanon has produced a number of gifted young artists who have shown a refreshing readiness to experiment with new expressive forms. Some Lebanese are active in international opera, theatre companies, and television and movie productions, whereas others are intent on creating a wider audience for classical Arabic

The ancient ruins of Baalbek remain a vibrant cultural centre, hosting the Baalbek International Festival with rock legends such as Deep Purple. Joseph Barrak/AFP/Getty Images

music and theatre. Some artists have remained cultural staples for many years. With a career spanning several decades, the immensely popular Lebanese singer Fairuz (Fayrūz) remains a well-known vocalist and a treasured cultural icon.

The cultural awakening encouraged the revival of national folk arts, particularly song, *dabkah* (the national dance), and *zajal* (folk poetry), and the refinement of traditional crafts.

In the 19th century, Lebanese linguists were in the vanguard of the Arabic literary awakening. In more recent times, writers of the calibre of Khalil Gibran, Georges Shehade, Michel Chiha, and Hanan al-Shaykh have been widely translated and have reached an international audience.

Khalil Gibran

(b. January 6, 1883, Bsharrī, Lebanon—d. April 10, 1931, New York, N.Y., U.S.)

Khalil Gibran (also spelled Jibran) was a Lebanese-American philosophical essayist, novelist, poet, and artist.

Having received his primary education in Beirut, Gibran immigrated with his parents to Boston in 1895. He returned to Lebanon in 1898 and studied in Beirut, where he excelled in the Arabic language. On his return to Boston in 1903, he published his first literary essays. Four years later, he met Mary Haskell, who was to be his benefactor all his life and who made it possible for him to study art in Paris. In 1912 Gibran settled in New York City and devoted himself to writing literary essays and short stories, both in Arabic and in English, and painting.

Gibran's literary and artistic output is highly romantic in outlook and was influenced by the Bible, Friedrich Nietzsche, and William Blake. His writings in both languages, which deal with such themes as love, death, nature, and a longing for the homeland, are brimming with lyrical outpourings and are expressive of Gibran's deeply religious and mystic nature.

Gibran's principal works in Arabic are: *'Arāʾis al-Murūj* (1910; *Nymphs of the Valley*); *Damʿah wa Ibtisāmah* (1914; *A Tear and a Smile*); *Al-Arwāḥ al-Mutamarridah* (1920; *Spirits Rebellious*); *Al-Ajniḥah al-Mutakassirah* (1922; *The Broken Wings*); *Al-'Awāṣif* (1923; *The Storms*); and *Al-Mawākib* (1923; *The Procession*), poems. His principal works in English are *The Madman* (1918), *The Forerunner* (1920), *The Prophet* (1923), *Sand and Foam* (1926), and *Jesus, the Son of Man* (1928).

CULTURAL INSTITUTIONS

While for a time cultural life in Lebanon was predominantly centred around universities and affiliated institutions, there has been an impressive proliferation of cultural activities under other auspices. Beirut has several museums and a number of private libraries, learned societies, and research institutions. The National Museum houses a collection of artifacts from Phoenician, Hellenistic, Roman, and Byzantine eras, and the National Library of Lebanon, closed in 1979 because of the civil war, began undergoing restorations in the early 21st century.

SPORTS AND RECREATION

Football (soccer) is among the most popular sports in Lebanon, although basketball is also favoured. Weight lifting has been popular with many Lebanese athletes since the mid-20th century, and the country has traditionally sent weight lifters to international competitions with some regularity. Participation in outdoor activities has also gained momentum. Lebanon has several well-equipped ski resorts, and downhill skiing is popular among the wealthy, while windsurfing and kayaking are favoured pastimes among the younger generation. The untamed peaks and breathtaking scenery of the Lebanon Mountains make hiking expeditions and mountain biking quite popular.

Lebanon sent a delegation of officials to the 1936 Summer Olympics in Berlin, paving the way for the formation in 1947 of the Lebanese Olympic Committee, which was acknowledged by the International Olympic Committee the following year. Since then, Lebanon has participated regularly in both the Summer and Winter Games. Lebanon has also hosted various competitions, including the Pan-Arab Games in 1997 and the Asian Cup in 2000.

MEDIA AND PUBLISHING

Lebanon has long had a strong print media tradition. The country's major Arabic papers include *Al-Nahār* and *Al-Safīr*; other publications include a French-language newspaper, *L'Orient–Le Jour*, and *The Daily Star*, an English daily. While Lebanon's print media has been vulnerable to a certain degree of political influence, the country's press nevertheless remains among the freest and most lively in the Arab world.

The relative independence of the print media contrasts sharply with the relatively high degree of regulation exercised by the government over audiovisual media. Television and radio broadcasting stations (especially those that air political news and commentary) are more heavily influenced by the government. Among these are television stations such as Télé-Liban, the official government station, as well as Future Television and the National Broadcasting Network. Additionally, there are numerous stations that feature music and general entertainment programs.

CHAPTER 10

Lebanon: Past and Present

The evidence of tools found in caves along the coast of what is now Lebanon shows that the area was inhabited from the Paleolithic Period (Old Stone Age) through the Neolithic Period (New Stone Age). Village life followed the domestication of plants and animals (the Neolithic Revolution, after about 10,000 BCE), with Byblos (modern Jbail) apparently taking the lead. At this site also appear the first traces in Lebanon of pottery and metallurgy (first copper, then bronze, an alloy of tin and copper) by the 4th millennium BCE.

The Obelisk Temple at Byblos, Lebanon. Ronald Sheridan

Byblos

Byblos (modern Jbail or Jubayl, biblical Gebal) is an ancient seaport, the site of which is located on the coast of the Mediterranean Sea, about 20 miles (30 km) north of the modern city of Beirut. It is one of the oldest continuously inhabited towns in the world. The name Byblos is Greek. Papyrus received its early Greek name (*byblos*, *byblinos*) from its being exported to the Aegean through Byblos. Hence the English word *bible* is derived from *byblos* as "the (papyrus) book."

Modern archaeological excavations have revealed that Byblos was occupied at least by the Neolithic Period (New Stone Age; *c.* 8000–*c.* 4000 BCE) and that during the 4th millennium BCE an extensive settlement developed there. Because Byblos was the chief harbour for the export of cedar and other valuable wood to Egypt, it soon became a great trading centre. It was called Kubna in ancient Egyptian and Gubla in Akkadian, the language of Assyria. Egyptian monuments and inscriptions found on the site attest to close relations with the Nile River Valley throughout the second half of the 2nd millennium. During Egypt's 12th dynasty (1938–1756 BCE), Byblos again became an Egyptian dependency, and the chief goddess of the city, Baalat ("The Mistress"), with her well-known temple at Byblos, was worshiped in Egypt. After the collapse of the Egyptian New Kingdom in the 11th century BCE, Byblos became the foremost city of Phoenicia.

The Phoenician alphabet was developed at Byblos, and the site has yielded almost all of the known early Phoenician inscriptions, most of them dating from the 10th century BCE. By that time, however, the Sidonian kingdom, with its capital at Tyre, had become dominant in Phoenicia, and Byblos, though it flourished into Roman times, never recovered its former supremacy. The Crusaders captured the town in 1103 and called it Gibelet. They built a castle there (using stone from earlier structures) but were driven out by the Ayyūbid sultan Saladin in 1189. The town subsequently sank into obscurity.

The ancient ruins of Byblos were rediscovered by the French historian Ernest Renan, who led a survey of the area. Systematic excavations were begun there by Pierre Montet in 1921. In the mid-1920s Maurice Dunand resumed the work and continued it until the mid-1970s. The ruins today consist of the Crusader fortifications and gate; a Roman colonnade and small theatre; Phoenician ramparts, three major temples, and a necropolis; and remains of Neolithic dwellings. Byblos was designated a UNESCO World Heritage site in 1984.

Present-day Jbail is adjacent to the archaeological site, extending from there to the waterfront area. Tourism is a major component of the local economy. In addition to the ruins, other notable attractions are the Church of St. John the Baptist, portions of which date to the early Crusader period, and a wax museum (opened 1970) dedicated to the area's history and rural Lebanese life.

PHOENICIA

The Phoenicians, indistinguishable from the Canaanites of Palestine, probably arrived in the land that became Phoenicia (a Greek term applied to the coast of Lebanon) about 3000 BCE. Herodotus and other classical writers preserve a tradition that they came from the coast of the Erythraean Sea (i.e., the Persian Gulf), but in fact nothing certain is known of their original homeland. Except at Byblos, no excavations have produced any information concerning the 3rd millennium in Phoenicia before the advent of the Phoenicians.

RELATIONS WITH EGYPT

Commercial and religious connections with Egypt, probably by sea, are attested from the Egyptian 4th dynasty (*c.* 2575–*c.* 2465 BCE). The earliest artistic representations of Phoenicians are found at Memphis, in a damaged relief of Pharaoh Sahure of the 5th dynasty (mid-25th to early 24th century BCE). This shows the arrival of an Asiatic princess to be the pharaoh's bride. Her escort is a fleet of seagoing ships, probably of the type known to the Egyptians as "Byblos ships," manned by crews of Asiatics, evidently Phoenicians.

Byblos was destroyed by fire about 2150 BCE, probably by the invading Amorites. The Amorites rebuilt on the site, and a period of close contact with Egypt was begun. Costly gifts were given by the pharaohs to those Phoenician and Syrian princes, such as the rulers of Ugarit and Katna, who were loyal to Egypt. Whether this attests to Egypt's political dominion over Phoenicia at this time or simply to strong diplomatic and commercial relations is not entirely clear.

In the 18th century BCE new invaders, the Hyksos, destroyed Amorite rule in Byblos and, passing on to Egypt, brought the Middle Kingdom to an end (*c.* 1630 BCE). Little is known about the Hyksos' origin, but they seem to have been ethnically mixed, including a considerable Semitic element, because the Phoenician deities El, Baal, and Anath figured in their pantheon. The rule of the Hyksos in Egypt was brief and their cultural achievement slight, but in this period the links with Phoenicia and Syria were strengthened by the presence of Hyksos aristocracies throughout the region. Pharaoh Ahmose I expelled the Hyksos about 1539 BCE and instituted the New Kingdom policy of conquest in Palestine and Syria. In his annals, Ahmose records capturing oxen from the Fenkhw, a term here perhaps referring to the Phoenicians. In the annals of the greatest Egyptian conqueror, Thutmose III (ruled *c.* 1479–26 BCE), the coastal plain of Lebanon, called Djahy, is described as rich with fruit, wine, and grain. Of particular importance to the New Kingdom pharaohs was the timber, notably cedar, of the Lebanese forests. A temple relief at Karnak depicts the chiefs of Lebanon felling cedars for the Egyptian officers of Seti I (*c.* 1300 BCE).

Fuller information about the state of Phoenicia in the 14th century BCE comes from the Amarna letters, diplomatic texts belonging to the Egyptian foreign office, written in cuneiform and found at Tell el-Amarna in Middle Egypt. These archives reveal that the land of Retenu (Syria-Palestine) was divided into three administrative districts, each under an Egyptian governor. The northernmost district (Amurru) included the coastal region from Ugarit to Byblos, the central district (Upi) included the southern Bekaa Valley and Anti-Lebanon Mountains, and the third district (Canaan) included all of Palestine from the Egyptian border to Byblos. Also among the letters are many documents addressed by the subject princes of Phoenicia and their Egyptian governors to the pharaoh. It was a time of much political unrest. The Hittites from central Anatolia were invading Syria. Nomads from the desert supported the invasion, and many of the local chiefs were ready to seize the opportunity to throw off the yoke of Egypt. The tablets that reveal this state of affairs are written in the language and script of Babylonia (i.e., Akkadian) and thus show the extent to which Babylonian culture had penetrated Palestine and Phoenicia. At the same time they illustrate the closeness of the relations between the Canaanite towns (i.e., those in Palestine) and the dominant power of Egypt.

After the reign of Akhenaton (Amenhotep IV; ruled 1353–36 BCE), that power collapsed altogether, but his successors attempted to recover it, and Ramses II (ruled 1279–13 BCE) reconquered Phoenicia as far as the Al-Kalb River. In the reign of Ramses III (1187–56 BCE), many great changes began to occur as a result of the invasion of Syria by peoples from Asia Minor and Europe. The successors of Ramses III lost their hold over Canaan, and the 21st dynasty no longer intervened in the affairs of Syria. In *The Story of Wen-Amon*, a tale of an Egyptian religious functionary sent to Byblos to secure cedar about 1100 BCE, the episode of the functionary's inhospitable reception shows the extent of the decline of Egypt's authority in Phoenicia at this time. Sheshonk (Shishak) I, the founder of the 22nd dynasty, endeavoured about 928 BCE to assert the ancient supremacy of Egypt. His successes, however, were not lasting, and, as is clear from the Old Testament, the power of Egypt thereafter became ineffective.

Phoenicia as a Colonial and Commercial Power

Kingship appears to have been the oldest form of Phoenician government. The royal houses claimed divine descent, and the king could not be chosen outside their members. His power, however, was limited by that of the merchant families, who wielded great influence in public affairs. Associated with the king was a council of elders; such at least was the case at Byblos, Sidon, and perhaps Tyre. During Nebuchadnezzar II's reign (*c.* 605–*c.* 561 BCE), a republic took the place of the monarchy at Tyre, and the government was administered by a succession of suffetes (judges). Suffetes held office for short terms, and in one instance two ruled together for six years. Much later, in the 3rd century BCE, an inscription from Tyre also mentions a suffete. Carthage was governed by two suffetes, and these officers are frequently named in connection with the Carthaginian colonies. But this does not justify any inference that Phoenicia itself had such magistrates. Under the Persians a federal bond was formed linking Sidon, Tyre, and Aradus. Federation on a larger scale was never possible in Phoenicia because no sense of political unity existed to bind the different states together.

Colonies

By the 2nd millennium BCE the Phoenicians had already extended their influence along the coast of the Levant by a series of settlements, some well known, some virtually nothing but names. Well known throughout history are

Joppa (Jaffa; later incorporated into Tel Aviv–Yafo, Israel) and Dor in the south. However, the earliest site known to possess important aspects of Phoenician culture outside the Phoenician homeland is Ugarit (Ra's Shamrah), about 6 miles (10 km) north of Latakia. The site was already occupied before the 4th millennium BCE, but the Phoenicians became prominent there only in the Egyptian 12th dynasty (1938–1756 BCE).

Evidence remains of two temples dedicated to the Phoenician gods Baal and Dagon, although the ruling family appears to have been of different, non-Phoenician extraction. The 15th century BCE shows strong cultural influences already established there from Cyprus and the world of Mycenaean Greece. A splendid archive of literary and administrative documents found at Ugarit from this period provides evidence of an early form of alphabetic script, arguably the most important Phoenician contribution to Western civilization. In the latter part of the 13th century BCE, a flood of land and sea raiders (the Sea Peoples) descended on the Levant coast, destroying many of the Phoenician cities and rolling onward to the frontier of Egypt, from which they were beaten back by the pharaoh Ramses III. Ugarit was destroyed, together with Aradus and Byblos, though the latter were afterward rebuilt. Though Sidon was destroyed only in part, its inhabitants fled to Tyre, which from this time was regarded as the principal city of Phoenicia and began its period of prosperity and expansion.

Tyre's first colony, Utica in North Africa, was founded perhaps as early as the 10th century BCE. It is likely that the expansion of the Phoenicians at the beginning of the 1st millennium BCE is to be connected with the alliance of Hiram of Tyre with Solomon of Israel in the second half of the 10th century BCE. In the following century, Phoenician presence in the north is shown by inscriptions at Samal (Zincirli Höyük) in eastern Cilicia and in the 8th century BCE at Karatepe in the Taurus Mountains, but there is no evidence of direct colonization. Both these cities acted as fortresses commanding the routes through the mountains to the mineral and other wealth of Anatolia.

Cyprus had Phoenician settlements by the 9th century BCE. Citium (biblical Kittim), known to the Greeks as Kition, in the southeast corner of the island, became the principal colony of the Phoenicians in Cyprus. Elsewhere in the Mediterranean, several smaller settlements were planted as stepping-stones along the route to Spain and its mineral wealth in silver and copper: early remains at Malta go back to the 7th century BCE and at Sulcis and Nora in Sardinia and Motya in Sicily perhaps a century earlier. According to Thucydides, the Phoenicians controlled a large part of the island but withdrew to the northwest corner under pressure from the Greeks. Modern scholars disbelieve this, however, and contend that the Phoenicians arrived only after the Greeks were established.

In North Africa the next site colonized after Utica was Carthage (near modern-day Tunis, Tunisia). Carthage in turn seems to have established (or in some cases reestablished) a number of settlements in Tunisia, Algeria, Morocco, the Balearic Islands, and southern Spain, eventually making this city the acknowledged leader of the western Phoenicians.

There is little factual evidence to confirm the presence of any settlement in Spain earlier than the 7th century BCE, or perhaps the 8th century, and many of these settlements should be viewed as Punic (Carthaginian) rather than Phoenician, though it is likely that the colonizing expeditions of the Carthaginians were supported by many emigrants from the Phoenician homeland. The tremendous colonial activity of the Phoenicians and Carthaginians was probably stimulated in the 8th–6th centuries BCE by the military blows that were wrecking the trade of the Phoenician homeland. Also, competition with the synchronous Greek colonization of the western Mediterranean cannot be ignored as a contributing factor.

In the 3rd century BCE Carthage, defeated by the Romans (in the First Punic War), embarked on a further imperialistic phase in Spain to recoup its losses. Rome responded, defeated Carthage a second time, and annexed Spain (Second Punic War). Finally, in 146 BCE, after a third war with Rome, Carthage suffered total destruction (Third Punic War). It was rebuilt as a Roman colony in 44 BCE. The ancient Phoenician language survived in use as a vernacular in some of the smaller cities of North Africa at least until the time of St. Augustine, bishop of Hippo (5th century CE).

Commerce

The mercantile role that tradition especially assigns to the Phoenicians was first developed on a considerable scale at the time of the Egyptian 18th dynasty. The position of Phoenicia, at a junction of both land and sea routes and under the protection of Egypt, favoured this development, and the discovery of the alphabet and its use and adaptation for commercial purposes assisted the rise of a mercantile society. A fresco in an Egyptian tomb of the 18th dynasty depicts seven Phoenician merchant ships that had just put in at an Egyptian port to sell their goods, including the distinctive Canaanite wine jars in which wine, a drink foreign to the Egyptians, was imported. *The Story of Wen-Amon* recounts the tale of a Phoenician merchant, Werket-el of Tanis in the Nile delta, who was described as the owner of 50 ships that sailed between Tanis and Sidon. The Sidonians are also famous in the poems of Homer as craftsmen, traders, pirates, and slave dealers. The biblical prophet Ezekiel, in a famous denunciation of the city of Tyre (Ezekiel 27–28), catalogs the vast extent of its commerce, covering most of the then-known world.

The exports of Phoenicia as a whole included particularly cedar and pine woods from Lebanon, fine linen from Tyre, Byblos, and Berytos, cloth dyed with the famous Tyrian purple (made from the snail *Murex*), embroideries from Sidon, metalwork and glass, glazed faience, wine, salt, and dried fish. The Phoenicians received in return raw materials such as papyrus, ivory, ebony, silk, amber, ostrich eggs, spices, incense, horses, gold, silver, copper, iron, tin, jewels, and precious stones.

In addition to these exports and imports, according to Herodotus's *History*, the Phoenicians also conducted an important transit trade, especially in the manufactured goods of Egypt and Babylonia. From the lands of the Euphrates and Tigris, regular trade routes led to the Mediterranean. In Egypt the Phoenician merchants soon gained a foothold, where they alone were able to maintain a profitable trade in the anarchic times of the 22nd and 23rd dynasties (*c.* 950–*c.* 715 BCE). Herodotus also observed that, though there were never any regular colonies of Phoenicians in Egypt, the Tyrians had a quarter of their own in Memphis and the Arabian caravan trade in perfume, spices, and incense passed through Phoenician hands on its way to Greece and the West.

The Phoenicians were not mere passive peddlers in art or commerce. Their achievement in history was a positive contribution, even if it was only that of an intermediary. For example, the extent of the debt of Greece alone to Phoenicia may be fully measured by its adoption, probably in the 8th century BCE, of the Phoenician alphabet with little variation (along with Semitic loanwords), by characteristically Phoenician decorative motifs on pottery and by architectural paradigms, and by the universal use in Greece of the Phoenician standards of weights and measures.

Navigation and Seafaring

Essential for the establishment of commercial supremacy was the Phoenician skill in navigation and seafaring. The Phoenicians are credited with the discovery and use of Polaris (the North Star). Fearless and patient navigators, they ventured into regions where no one else dared to go, and always, with an eye to their monopoly, they carefully guarded the secrets of their trade routes and discoveries and their knowledge of winds and currents. According to Herodotus, Pharaoh Necho II (ruled 610–595 BCE) organized the Phoenician circumnavigation of Africa (*History*, Book IV, chapter 42). Hanno, a Carthaginian, led another in the mid-5th century. The Carthaginians seem to have reached the island of Corvo in the Azores, and they may even have reached Britain, for many Carthaginian coins have been found there.

Assyrian and Babylonian Domination of Phoenicia

Between the withdrawal of Egyptian rule in Syria and the western advance of Assyria, there was an interval during which the city-states of Phoenicia owned no suzerain. Byblos had kings of its own, among them Ahiram, Abi-baal, and Ethbaal (Ittoba'al) in the 10th century, as excavations have shown. The history of this time period is mainly a history of Tyre, which not only rose to a hegemony among the Phoenician states but also founded colonies beyond the seas. Unfortunately, the native historical records of the Phoenicians have not survived, but it is clear from the Bible that the Phoenicians lived on friendly terms with the Israelites. In the 10th century BCE Hiram, king of Tyre, built the Temple of Solomon at Jerusalem in return for rich gifts of oil, wine, and territory. In the following century Ethbaal of Tyre married his daughter Jezebel to Ahab, king of Israel, and Jezebel's daughter in turn married the king of Judah.

In the 9th century, however, the independence of Phoenicia was increasingly threatened by the advance of Assyria. In 868 BCE Ashurnasirpal II reached the Mediterranean and exacted tribute from the Phoenician cities. His son, Shalmaneser III, took tribute from the Tyrians and Sidonians and established a supremacy over Phoenicia (at any rate, in theory), which was acknowledged by occasional payments of tribute to him and his successors. In 734 BCE Tiglath-pileser III in his western campaign established his authority over Byblos, Arados, and Tyre. A fresh invasion by Shalmaneser V took place in 725 when he was on his way to Samaria, and in 701 Sennacherib, facing a rebellion of Philistia, Judah, and Phoenicia, drove out and deposed Luli, identified as king of both Sidon and Tyre. In 678 Sidon rebelled against the Assyrians, who marched down and annihilated the city, rebuilding it on the mainland. Sieges of Tyre took place in 672 and 668, but the city resisted both, only submitting in the later years of Ashurbanipal.

During the period of Neo-Babylonian power, which followed the fall of Nineveh in 612 BCE, the pharaohs made attempts to seize the Phoenician and Palestinian seaboard. Nebuchadnezzar II, king of Babylon, having sacked Jerusalem, marched against Phoenicia and besieged Tyre, but it held out successfully for 13 years, after which it capitulated, seemingly on favourable terms.

Persian Period

Phoenicia passed from the suzerainty of the Babylonians to that of their conquerors, the Persian Achaemenian dynasty, in 538 BCE. Not surprisingly, the Phoenicians turned as loyal supporters to the Persians, who had overthrown their oppressors and reopened to them the trade of the East. Lebanon, Syria-Palestine, and Cyprus were organized as the fifth satrapy (province) of the Persian Empire. At the time of Xerxes I's invasion of Greece (480 BCE), Sidon was considered the principal city of Phoenicia. The ships of Sidon were considered the finest part of Xerxes's fleet, and its king ranked next to Xerxes and before the king of Tyre. (Phoenician coins have been used to supplement historical sources on the period. From the reign of Darius I [522–486 BCE], the Persian monarchs had allowed their satraps and vassal states to coin silver and copper money. Arados, Byblos, Sidon, and Tyre therefore issued coinage of their own.) In the 4th century Tyre and later Sidon revolted against the Persian king. The revolt was suppressed in 345 BCE.

GREEK AND ROMAN PERIODS

In 332 BCE Tyre resisted Alexander the Great in a siege of eight months. Alexander finally captured the city by driving a mole into the sea from the mainland to the island. As a result, Tyre, the inhabitants of which were largely sold into slavery, lost all importance, soon being replaced in the leadership of the regional markets by Alexandria, the conqueror's newly founded city in Egypt. In the Hellenistic Age (323–30 BCE) the cities of Phoenicia became the prize for the competing Macedonian dynasties, controlled first by the Ptolemies of Egypt in the 3rd century BCE and then by the Seleucid dynasty of Syria in the 2nd century and early decades of the 1st century BCE. The Seleucids apparently permitted a good measure of autonomy to the Phoenician cities. Tigranes II (the Great) of Armenia brought an end to the Seleucid dynasty in 83 BCE and extended his realm to Mount Lebanon. The

Romans eventually intervened to restore Seleucid sovereignty, but, when anarchy prevailed, they imposed peace and assumed direct rule in 64 BCE.

Phoenicia was incorporated into the Roman province of Syria, though Aradus, Sidon, and Tyre retained self-government. Berytus (Beirut), relatively obscure up to this point, rose to prominence by virtue of Augustus's grant of Roman colonial status and by the lavish building program financed by Herod the Great (and in turn by his grandson and great-grandson). Under the Severan dynasty (193–235 CE) Sidon, Tyre, and probably Heliopolis (Baalbek) also received colonial status. Under this dynasty the province of Syria was partitioned into two parts: Syria Coele ("Hollow Syria"), comprising a large region loosely defined as north and east Syria, and Syria Phoenice in the southwestern region, which included not only coastal Phoenicia but also the territory beyond the mountains and into the Syrian Desert. Under the provincial reorganization of the Eastern Roman emperor Theodosius II in the early 5th century CE, Syria Phoenice was expanded into two provinces: Phoenice Prima (Maritima), basically ancient Phoenicia; and Phoenice Secunda (Libanesia), an area extending to Mount Lebanon on the west and deep into the Syrian Desert on the east. Phoenice Secunda included the cities of Emesa (its capital), Heliopolis, Damascus, and Palmyra.

During the period of the Roman Empire, the native Phoenician language died out in Lebanon and was replaced by Aramaic as the vernacular. Latin, the language of the soldiers and administrators, in turn fell before Greek, the language of letters of the eastern Mediterranean, by the 5th century CE. Lebanon produced a number of important writers in Greek, most notably Philo of Byblos (64–141) and, in the 3rd century, Porphyry of Tyre and Iamblichus of Chalcis in Syria Coele. Porphyry played a key role in disseminating the Neoplatonic philosophy of his master, Plotinus, which would influence both pagan and Christian thought in the later Roman Empire.

In many respects, the two most important cities of Lebanon during the time of the Roman Empire were Heliopolis and Berytus. At Heliopolis the Roman emperors, particularly the Severans, constructed a monumental temple complex, the most spectacular elements of which were the Temple of Jupiter Heliopolitanus and the Temple of Bacchus. Conversely, Berytus became the seat of the most famous provincial school of Roman law. The school, which probably was founded by Septimius Severus, lasted until the destruction of Berytus itself by a sequence of earthquakes, a tidal wave, and fire in the mid-6th century. Two of Rome's most famous jurists, Papinian and Ulpian, both natives of Lebanon, taught as professors at the law school under the Severans. Their judicial opinions constitute well over one-third of the Pandects (Digest) contained in the great compilation of Roman law commissioned by the emperor Justinian I in the 6th century CE.

In 608–609 the Persian king Khosrow II pillaged Syria and Lebanon and reorganized the area into a new satrapy, excluding only Phoenicia Maritima. Between 622 and 629 the Byzantine emperor Heraclius mounted an offensive and restored Syria-Lebanon to his empire. This success was short-lived. In the 630s Muslim Arabs conquered Palestine and Lebanon, and the old Phoenician cities offered only token resistance to the invader.

LEBANON IN THE MIDDLE AGES

The population of Lebanon did not begin to take its present form until the 7th century CE. At some time in the Byzantine period, a military group of uncertain origin, the Mardaïtes, established themselves in the north among the indigenous population. From the 7th century onward

Maronite Church

The Maronite church is one of the largest Eastern-rite communities of the Roman Catholic Church, prominent especially in modern Lebanon. It is the only Eastern-rite church that has no non-Catholic or Orthodox counterpart. The Maronites trace their origins to St. Maron, or Maro (Arabic: Mārūn), a Syrian hermit of the late 4th and early 5th centuries, and St. John Maron, or Joannes Maro (Arabic: Yūḥanna Mārūn), patriarch of Antioch in 685–707, under whose leadership the invading Byzantine armies of Justinian II were routed in 684, making the Maronites a fully independent people.

Though their traditions assert that the Maronites were always orthodox Christians in union with the Roman see, there is evidence that for centuries they were Monothelites, followers of the heretical doctrine of Sergius, patriarch of Constantinople, who affirmed that there was a divine but no human will in Christ. According to the medieval bishop William of Tyre, the Maronite patriarch sought union with the Latin patriarch of Antioch in 1182. A definitive consolidation of the union, however, did not come until the 16th century, brought about largely through the work of the Jesuit John Eliano. In 1584 Pope Gregory XIII founded the Maronite College in Rome, which flourished under Jesuit administration into the 20th century and became a training centre for scholars and leaders.

Hardy, martial mountaineers, the Maronites valiantly preserved their liberty and folkways. The Muslim caliphate could not absorb them, and two caliphs of the Umayyad dynasty paid them tribute. Under the rule of the Ottoman Turks, the Maronites maintained their religion and customs under the protection of France, largely because of their geographic isolation. In the 19th century, however, the Ottoman government incited a neighbouring mountain people of Lebanon, the Druzes, against the Maronites, a policy that culminated in the great Maronite massacre of 1860. As a result of this incident, the Maronites achieved formal autonomy within the Ottoman Empire under a nonnative Christian ruler. In 1920, following the dissolution of the Ottoman Empire, the Maronites of Lebanon became self-ruling under French protection. Since the establishment of a fully independent Lebanon in 1943, they have constituted one of the major religious groups in the country. The government is run by a coalition of Christian, Muslim, and Druze parties, but the president is always Maronite.

The immediate spiritual head of the Maronite church after the pope is the "patriarch of Antioch and all the East," residing in Bkirkī, near Beirut. The church retains the ancient West Syrian liturgy, even though the vernacular tongue of the Maronites is Arabic. Contact with Rome has been close and cordial, but it was not until after the Second Vatican Council that the Maronites were freed of papal efforts to Latinize their rite. French Jesuits conducted the University of St. Joseph, at Beirut.

Maronites are also found in southern Europe and North and South America, having emigrated in the 19th century under the pressure of persecutions. The émigrés keep their own liturgy and have their own clergy, some of whom are married.

another group entered the country, the Maronites, a Christian community adhering to the monothelite doctrine. Forced by persecution to leave their homes in northern Syria, they settled in the northern part of the Lebanon Mountains and absorbed the Mardaïtes and indigenous peasants to form the present Maronite church. Originally Syriac-speaking, they gradually adopted the Arabic language while keeping Syriac for liturgical purposes. In south Lebanon, Arab tribesmen came in after the Muslim conquest of Syria in the 7th century and settled among the indigenous people. In the 11th century many were converted to the Druze faith, an esoteric offshoot of Shīʿite Islam. South Lebanon became the headquarters of the faith. Groups of Shīʿite Muslims settled on the northern and southern fringes of the mountains and in the Bekaa Valley. In the coastal towns the population became mainly Sunni Muslim, but in town and country alike there remained considerable numbers of Christians of various sects. In the course of time, virtually all sections of the population adopted Arabic, the language of the Muslim states in which Lebanon was included.

Beirut and Mount Lebanon were ruled by the Umayyad dynasty (661–750) as part of the district of Damascus. In spite of the occasional rising by the Maronites, Lebanon provided naval forces to the Umayyads in their interminable warfare with the Byzantines. The 8th-century Beirut legist al-Awzāʿī established a school of Islamic law that heavily influenced Lebanon and Syria. From the 9th to the 11th century, coastal Lebanon was usually under the sway of independent Egyptian Muslim dynasties, although the Byzantine Empire attempted to gain portions of the north.

At the end of the 11th century, Lebanon became a part of the Crusader states, the north being incorporated in the county of Tripoli, the south in the kingdom of Jerusalem. The Maronite church began to accept papal supremacy while keeping its own patriarch and liturgy.

In spite of the strong fortresses of the Crusaders, a Muslim reconquest of Lebanon began, under the leadership of Egypt, with the fall of Beirut to the famous sultan Saladin in 1187. Mongol raids against the Bekaa Valley were defeated. Lebanon became part of the Mamlūk state of Egypt and Syria in the 1280s and '90s and was divided between several provinces. Mamlūk rule, which allowed limited local autonomy to regional leaders, encouraged commerce. The coastal cities, especially Tripoli, flourished, and the people of the interior were left largely free to manage their own affairs.

OTTOMAN PERIOD

Expansion of the Ottoman Empire began in the area under Selim I (ruled 1512–20). He defeated the Mamlūks in 1516–17 and added Lebanon (as part of Mamlūk Syria and Egypt) to his empire. Between the 16th and 18th centuries, Ottoman Lebanon evolved a social and political system of its own. Ottoman Aleppo or Tripoli governed the north, Damascus the centre, and Sidon (after 1660) the south. Coastal Lebanon and the Bekaa Valley were usually ruled more directly from Constantinople (modern-day Istanbul, Turkey), the Ottoman capital, while Mount Lebanon enjoyed semiautonomous status. The population took up its present position: the Shīʿites were driven out of the north but increased their strength in the south; many Druze moved from south Lebanon to Jebel Druze (Jabal Al-Durūz) in southern Syria; Maronite peasants, increasing in numbers, moved south into districts mainly populated by Druze. Monasteries acquired more land and wealth. In all parts of the mountains there grew up families of notables who controlled the land and established a feudal relation with the cultivators; some were Christian, some Druze, who were politically dominant. From them arose the house of Maʿn, which established a princedom over the whole of Mount Lebanon and was accepted by Christians and Druze alike. Fakhr al-Dīn II ruled most of Lebanon from 1593 to 1633 and encouraged commerce. When the house of Maʿn died out in 1697, the notables elected as prince a member of the Shihāb family, who were Sunni Muslims but with Druze followers, and this family ruled until 1842. Throughout this period European influence was growing. European trading colonies were established in Saïda and other coastal towns, mainly to trade in silk, the major Lebanese export from the 17th to the 20th century. French political influence was great, particularly among the Maronites, who formally united with the Roman Catholic Church in 1736.

The 19th century was marked by economic growth, social change, and political crisis. The growing Christian population moved southward and into the towns, and

Bashīr Shihāb II

(b. 1767, Ghazīr, Lebanon—d. 1850, Istanbul, Turkey)

Bashīr Shihāb II was a Lebanese prince who established hegemony over Lebanon in the first half of the 19th century and ruled it under Ottoman and, later, Egyptian suzerainty from 1788 to 1840.

Although born into the princely Shihāb family, Bashīr grew up in poverty but married into great wealth. In 1788 the Lebanese emir was forced to abdicate, and the local nobility selected Bashīr to fill the post. As emir, Bashīr had to raise tribute for Aḥmad al-Jazzār, an official nominated by the Ottoman sultan to administer the district of Lebanon. After the death of al-Jazzār (1804), the financial demands were much less severe, and Bashīr was able to consolidate his position. With the notable exception of the Jumblatts, he destroyed the power of the Druze princes, on whose support Lebanese emirs had usually depended.

In 1821 Bashīr provided military support to the pasha of Acre, who tried to draw the city of Damascus under his authority. But the Ottoman sultan declared the pasha a rebel, and Bashīr fled to Egypt. Later, after the pasha was pardoned, Bashīr returned to Lebanon, where, in his absence, the Druze sheikh Bashīr Jumblatt had plotted against him. By having Jumblatt killed, Bashīr became the undisputed ruler of Lebanon.

When Muḥammad ʿAlī occupied the Fertile Crescent (exclusive of Iraq) in the 1830s, Bashīr cooperated fully with the new regime in establishing order. In 1837 he armed 4,000 Christians to put down a rebellion that the Druzes had begun when threatened with conscription (hitherto Lebanese rulers had avoided direct clashes between the two groups). Two years later Bashīr tried to disarm the same Christians whom he had previously armed, clearly as a prelude to their conscription. The Christians were determined to resist, even if it meant cooperating with the Druzes. A Druze and Christian rebellion against Bashīr broke out in June 1840, supported by the British, who were intent on driving Muḥammad ʿAlī out of the Fertile Crescent. Bashīr could not reassert his authority, and in October he was forced into exile in Malta.

toward the end of the century many of these Christians immigrated to North America, South America, and Egypt. French Catholic and American Protestant mission schools, as well as schools of the local communities, multiplied. In 1866 the American mission established the Syrian Protestant College (now the American University of Beirut), and in 1875 the Jesuits started the Université Saint-Joseph. Such schools produced a literate class, particularly among the Christians, that found employment as professionals. Beirut became a great international port, and its merchant houses established connections with Egypt, the Mediterranean countries, and England.

The growth of the Christian communities upset the traditional balance of Lebanon. The Shihāb princes inclined more and more toward them, and part of the family indeed became Maronites. The greatest of them, Bashīr II (ruled 1788–1840), after establishing his power with the help of Druze notables, tried to weaken them. When the Egyptian troops of Ibrāhīm Pasha occupied Lebanon and Syria in 1831, Bashīr formed an alliance with him to limit the power of the ruling families and to preserve his own power. But Egyptian rule was ended by Anglo-Ottoman intervention, aided by a popular rising in 1840, and Bashīr was deposed. With him the princedom virtually ended. His weak successor was deposed by the Ottomans in 1842, and from that time relations grew worse between the Maronites, led by their patriarch, and the Druze, trying to retain their traditional supremacy. The French supported the Maronites and the British supported a section of the Druze, while the Ottoman government encouraged the collapse of the traditional structure, which would enable it to impose its own direct authority. The conflict culminated in the massacre of Maronites by the Druze in 1860. The complacent attitude of the Ottoman authorities led to direct French intervention on behalf of the Christians. The powers jointly imposed the Organic Regulation of 1861 (modified in 1864), which gave Mount Lebanon, the axial mountain region, autonomy under a Christian governor appointed by the Ottoman sultan, assisted by a council representing the various communities. Mount Lebanon prospered under this regime until World War I (1914–18), when the Ottoman government placed it under strict control, similar to that already established for the coast and the Bekaa Valley.

French Mandate

At the end of World War I, Lebanon was occupied by Allied forces and placed under a French military administration. In 1920 Beirut and other coastal towns, the Bekaa Valley, and certain other districts were added to the autonomous territory Mount Lebanon as defined in 1861 to form Greater Lebanon (Grand Liban; subsequently called the Lebanese Republic). In 1920 the Conference of San Remo gave the mandate for Lebanon and Syria to France. The Maronites, strongly pro-French by tradition, welcomed this, and during the next 20 years, while France held the mandate, the Maronites were favoured. The expansion of prewar Lebanon into Greater Lebanon, however, changed the balance of the population. Although the Maronites were the largest single element, they no longer formed a majority. The population was more or less equally divided between Christians and Muslims, and a large section of it wanted neither to be ruled by France nor to be part of an independent Lebanon but rather to form part of a larger Syrian or Arab state. To ease tensions between the communities, the constitution of 1926 provided that each should be equitably represented in public offices. Thus, by convention the president of the republic was normally a Maronite, the prime minister a Sunni Muslim, and the speaker of the chamber a Shīʿite Muslim.

Under French administration, public utilities and communications were improved, and education was expanded (although higher education was left almost wholly in the hands of religious bodies). Beirut prospered as a centre of trade with surrounding countries, but agriculture was depressed by the decline of the silk industry and the worldwide economic depression. As the middle class of Beirut grew and a real, if fragile, sense of common national interest sprang up alongside communal loyalties, there also grew the desire for more independence. A Franco-Lebanese treaty of independence and friendship was signed in 1936 but was not ratified by the French government. Lebanon was controlled by the Vichy authorities after the fall of France in 1940 but was occupied by British and Free French troops in 1941. The Free French representative proclaimed the independence of Lebanon and Syria, which was underwritten by the British government. Because of their own precarious position, however, the Free French were unwilling to relax control. In 1943, however, they held elections, which resulted in victory for the Nationalists. Their leader, Bishara al-Khuri, was elected president. The new government passed legislation introducing certain constitutional changes that eliminated all traces of French influence, to which the French objected. On November 11, 1943, the president and almost the entire government were arrested by the French. This led to an insurrection, followed by British diplomatic intervention. The French restored the government and transferred powers to it. Although independence had been proclaimed on Novemebr 22, 1943, it was not until after another crisis in 1945 that an agreement was reached on a simultaneous withdrawal of British and French troops. This was completed by the end of 1946, and Lebanon became wholly independent. It had already become a member of the United Nations (UN) and the Arab League.

LEBANON AFTER INDEPENDENCE

For many years Lebanon maintained its parliamentary democracy, in spite of serious trials. The main problem for Lebanon was to implement the unwritten power-sharing National Pact of 1943 between the Christians and Muslims. In the early years of independence, so long as no urgent call for pan-Arab unity came from outside, the National Pact faced no serious strains.

Khuri Regime, 1943–52

Bishara al-Khuri, the Maronite president, closely cooperated with the Sunni leader Riad al-Sulh, who was premier most of the time. A temporary amendment of the constitution permitted the president, in 1949, a second six-year term. The parliamentary elections of 1947 were manipulated to produce a parliament favourable to the amendment. This, together with the open favouritism of the president toward his friends and the gross corruption he allegedly condoned, made Khuri increasingly unpopular after his reelection in 1949.

The military coup that overthrew the regime of Shukri al-Quwatli in Syria in March 1949 encouraged the opponents of Khuri in Lebanon. In July 1949 the Syrian Social Nationalist Party (SSNP; the Parti Populair Syrien) tried to overthrow the regime by force. The coup failed, and its leaders were seized and shot. The SSNP took its revenge by securing the assassination of Khuri's premier in 1951. The mounting opposition to the Khuri regime culminated in September 1952 in a general strike that forced his resignation. Camille Chamoun was elected by the parliament to succeed him.

Chamoun Regime and the 1958 Crisis

The presidency of Camille Chamoun coincided with the rise of Arab nationalist leader Gamal Abdel Nasser in Egypt. During the 1956 Suez Crisis, Chamoun earned Nasser's enmity by refusing to break off diplomatic relations with Britain and France, which had joined Israel in attacking Egypt. Chamoun was accused of seeking to align Lebanon with the Western-sponsored Central Treaty Organization, also known as the Baghdad Pact.

Matters came to a head following the parliamentary elections of 1957, which allegedly were manipulated to produce a parliament favourable to the reelection of Chamoun. When Syria entered into a union with Egypt—as the United Arab Republic—in February 1958, the Muslim opposition to Chamoun in Lebanon hailed the union as a triumph for Pan-Arabism, and there were widespread demands that Lebanon be associated in the union. In May a general strike was proclaimed, and the Muslims of Tripoli rose in armed insurrection. The insurrection spread, and the army was asked to take action against the insurgents. The commanding general, Fuad Chehab, refused to attack them for fear that the army, which was composed of Christians and Muslims, would split apart. The Chamoun government took the issue of external intervention to the UN, accusing the United Arab Republic of intervention, and UN observers were sent to Lebanon. When in July the pro-Western regime in Iraq was toppled in a coup, President Chamoun immediately requested U.S. military intervention, and on the following day U.S. Marines landed outside Beirut. The presence of

U.S. troops had little immediate effect on the internal situation, but the insurrection slowly faded out. Parliament turned to the commander of the army, General Chehab, as a compromise candidate to succeed Chamoun as his term ended. Rashid Karami became the new premier.

Chehabism: From Chehab to Hélou, 1958–76

The crisis had been resolved by compromise, and the Chehab regime was successful in maintaining the compromise and promoting the national unity of the Lebanese people. By his refusal as army commander to take offensive action against the insurgents in 1958, Chehab had earned the confidence of the Muslims. Once in power, he proceeded to allay long-standing Muslim grievances by associating Muslims more closely in the administration and by attending to neglected areas of Lebanon where Muslims predominated. Internal stability was further promoted by the maintenance of good relations with the United Arab Republic, which, even after the Syrian secession in 1961, remained highly popular with the Muslim Lebanese. The economic boom that had begun under the Chamoun regime as the result of the flight of capital from the unstable Arab world into Lebanon continued under the Chehab regime.

After stabilizing confessional relations, Chehab embarked upon a program of reform intended to strengthen the Lebanese state, the capabilities of which up until that time had been enormously weak. His main goal was to reduce some of the social and economic imbalances that had begun to emerge in Lebanese society and which were reflected in the political system by the dominance of the *zuʿamāʾ* (old semifeudal elites). Personnel reform legislation passed in 1959 called for an equality of appointments for Christians and Muslims to bureaucratic posts. His efforts to expand the state's role in the provision of social services were regarded by the traditional elites with suspicion, as this development competed with their own patronage networks. Through the establishment of state-run agencies such as the Litani River Authority aimed at improving the socioeconomic status of the relatively underserved (and largely Shīʿite) south of the country, Chehab also tried to enhance the role of the Lebanese state in development activities.

Charles Hélou, a former journalist and member of Khuri's Constitutional Bloc, was elected to succeed Chehab in 1964. Hélou's presidency, essentially a similar—if weaker—version of the Chehab administration, coincided with a period of great change in Lebanon that would lead to the outbreak of civil war in 1975. Combined with the country's oil boom, Chehab-era reforms set off a wave of tremendous socioeconomic change in Lebanon that led to dramatic increases in social mobility and urbanization, especially in Beirut. Like the country, however, the city failed to achieve a balanced integration of its various groups. Beirut became a reflection of Lebanon as a whole as each quarter took on a religious affiliation, and newcomers suffered from deep and growing social and economic contrasts with their more affluent neighbours. Freed from the control of their rural patrons and unintegrated into the urban social and political fabric, these migrants, relatively underprivileged compared with the wealthier urban classes of Beirut, soon emerged as a tremendous source of potential instability. By the mid-1970s a multitiered "poverty belt"—a ring of impoverished settlements largely populated by poorer rural migrants—had sprung up to encircle the city.

Social and political polarization in Lebanon was further increased by the movement of Palestinian guerrillas into Lebanon, particularly after the Jordanian campaign against the Palestinian militias and subsequent expulsion of the Palestine Liberation Organization (PLO) from Jordan in the early 1970s. After being forced from bases in Jordan, the Palestinians thought of Lebanon as their last refuge, and by 1973 roughly one-tenth of the population in Lebanon was Palestinian. Landless, mostly poor, and without political status, the Palestinians in Lebanon contributed to the polarization of Lebanese politics as they found common cause with those Lebanese who were poor, rural, and mainly Muslim. As socioeconomic alienation increasingly began to intersect with confessional grievances, and as the Palestinian presence in Lebanon began to essentially acquire the status of a "state within a state," Lebanon's delicate political balance began to unravel.

Civil War

The experiment in state building started by Chehab and continued by Hélou came to an end with the election of Suleiman Franjieh to the presidency in August 1970. Franjieh, a traditional Maronite clan leader from the Zghartā region of northern Lebanon, proved unable to shield the state from the conflicting forces lining up against it. The dramatic increase in social and political mobilization sparked by the growing presence of Palestinian guerrillas led to the emergence of various new social and political movements, including Mūsā al-Ṣadr's Ḥarakat al-Maḥrūmīn ("Movement of the Deprived"), and to the rise of numerous sectarian-based militias. Unable to maintain a monopoly of force, the Lebanese state apparatus was powerless to stop the increase in violence that was gradually destroying the country's fragile social and political fabric. On the eve of the civil war in the mid-1970s, the escalating violence had deepened the fault line between the Maronite Christian and Muslim communities, symbolized in turn by the increasing power of the Christian Phalangists, led by Pierre Gemayel, and the predominantly Muslim Lebanese National Movement (LNM), led by Kamal Jumblatt.

On April 13, 1975, the Phalangists attacked a bus of Palestinians en route to a refugee camp at Tall al-Zaʿtar, an attack that escalated into a more general battle between the Phalangists and the LNM. In the months that followed, the general destruction of the central market area of Beirut was marked by the emergence of a "green line" between Muslim West Beirut and Christian East Beirut, which persisted until the end of the civil war in 1990, with each side under the control of its respective militias. Lebanon witnessed the disintegration of many of its administrative apparatuses, including the army, which splintered into its various sectarian components.

In the midst of this violence, Elias Sarkis was elected president in May 1976. With the Christians on the defensive against the forces affiliated with the LNM, there appeared to be some opening for negotiations to patch up the fractured communal consensus. Sarkis's mediation efforts, however, were thwarted by two principal factors that continued to plague negotiation efforts throughout the civil war: the increasing interference of external actors in the Lebanese conflict and the emergence of power struggles within the various sectarian communities that ultimately militated against stable negotiations.

The first major intervention by an external actor in the Lebanese civil war was carried out by Syria. In spite of its earlier support for the PLO, Syria feared that an LNM-PLO victory would provoke Israeli intervention against the Palestinians and lead Syria into a confrontation with Israel, thereby complicating Syria's own interests. As a result, in June 1976 it launched a large-scale intervention to redress the emerging imbalance of power in favour of the Christians. Syria's intervention sparked a more active Israeli involvement in Lebanese affairs, in which Israel also intervened on behalf of the Christians, whom Israelis looked upon as their main ally in their fight against the PLO. Thus, Israel provided arms and finances to the Christians in the south of the country while the Palestinian forces (who by 1977 again enjoyed Syrian support) continued to conduct cross-border raids into Israel. In March 1978 Israel launched a major reprisal attack, sending troops into the south of Lebanon as far as the Līṭānī River. The resulting conflict led to the establishment of the UN Interim Force in Lebanon (UNIFIL)—a peacekeeping force meant to secure Israeli withdrawal and support the return of Lebanese authority in the south—as well as to the creation of the South Lebanese Army (SLA)—a militia led by Saʿd Haddad and armed and financed by Israel to function as a proxy militia under Lebanese Christian command.

The most significant Israeli intervention during the course of the Lebanese civil war, however, was the invasion that began on June 6, 1982. Although the stated goal of Israel was only to secure the territory north of its border with Lebanon so as to stop PLO raids, Israeli forces quickly progressed as far as Beirut's suburbs and laid siege to the capital, particularly to West Beirut. The invasion resulted in the eventual removal of PLO militia from Lebanon under the supervision of a multinational peacekeeping force, the transfer of the PLO headquarters to Tunis, Tunisia, and the temporary withdrawal of Syrian forces back to the Bekaa Valley. Galvanized by the Israeli invasion, a number of Shīʿite groups subsequently emerged, including Hezbollah, an Iranian-backed militia that led an insurgency campaign against Israeli troops.

In August 1982 Pierre Gemayel's son Bashir, the young Phalangist leader who had managed to unify the Maronite militias into the Lebanese Forces (LF), was elected to the presidency. In mid-September, however, three weeks after his election, Gemayel was assassinated in a bombing at the Phalangist headquarters. Two days later, Christian militiamen under the command of Elie Hobeika, permitted entry to the area by Israeli forces, retaliated by killing hundreds (estimates range from several hundreds to several thousands) of people in the Palestinian refugee camps of Sabra and Shatila. The election of Bashir's brother, Amin Gemayel, to the presidency in late September 1982 failed to temper the mounting violence as battles between the Christians and the Druze broke out in the traditionally Druze territory of the Shūf Mountains, resulting in numerous Christian fatalities. The Western peacekeeping forces that had been dispatched to Lebanon in 1982 likewise suffered heavy casualties, among them the destruction of the U.S. embassy by a car bomb in April 1983 and the suicide attacks on the U.S. and French troops of the multinational force stationed in Lebanon in October 1983, which hastened their withdrawal from Lebanon early the following year. By mid-1985 most of the Israeli troops had also withdrawn, leaving the proxy SLA in control of a buffer zone north of the international border in their wake.

Exacerbated by various foreign interventions, the Lebanese civil war descended into a complicated synthesis of inter- and intracommunal conflict characterized by the increasing fragmentation of the militias associated with each of the sectarian communities. The Phalangist-dominated LF fractured into various contending parties that were in turn challenged by the militias of the Franjieh and Chamoun families in the north and south of the country, respectively. Meanwhile, the Sunni community's militias were challenged by militias organized by Islamic fundamentalist groups, and the Shīʿite community experienced fierce divisions between the more clerical Hezbollah in the south and the more secular Amal ("Hope," also an acronym for Afwāj al-Muqāwamah al-Lubnāniyyah [Lebanese Resistance Detachments]) movement led by Nabbih Berri. The Palestinians in turn endured serious infighting between Fatah factions of the PLO that had begun to return to the country following the Israeli withdrawal.

Fueled by continuing foreign patronage, Lebanon between 1985 and 1989 descended into a "war society" as the various militias became increasingly involved in smuggling, extortion, and the arms and drug trades and began to lose their populist legitimacy. This period of disintegration was crystallized with the decline of many of the country's remaining institutions, and in 1987 the collapse of the Lebanese pound—which had demonstrated a surprising resiliency throughout the first 10 years of the war—led to a period of profound economic hardship and inflation. Furthermore, when Gemayel's term ended on September 22, 1988, parliament could not agree on the selection of a new president. As a result, Gemayel named General Michel Aoun, a Maronite and the head of what was left of the Lebanese Army, as acting prime minister moments before his own term expired, in spite of the continuing claim to that office by the Sunni incumbent, Salim al-Hoss. Lebanon thus had no president but two prime ministers, and two separate governments emerged in competition for legitimacy. In late November 1988, General Aoun was dismissed as commander in chief of the armed forces. Because of the continued loyalty of large portions of the military, however, Aoun was able to retain a de facto leadership. In February 1989 Aoun launched an offensive against the rival LF, and in March he declared a "war of liberation" in an attempt to expel the Syrian influence. In September 1989, following months of intense violence, Aoun accepted a cease-fire brokered by a tripartite committee made up of the leaders of Algeria, Morocco, and Saudi Arabia.

Michel Aoun vehemently opposed the Ṭāʾif Accord, concerned that it might allow Syria continued involvement in Lebanon. Joseph Barrak/AFP/Getty Images

On October 22, 1989, most members of the Lebanese parliament (last elected in 1972) met in Ṭā'if, Saudi Arabia, and accepted a constitutional reform package that restored consociational government in Lebanon in modified form. The power of the traditionally Maronite president was reduced in relation to those of the Sunni prime minister and the Shīʿite speaker of the National Assembly, and the division of parliamentary seats, cabinet posts, and senior administrative positions was adjusted to represent an equal ratio of Christian and Muslim officials. A commitment was made for the gradual elimination of confessionalism, and Lebanese independence was affirmed with a call for an end to foreign occupation in the south. The terms of the agreement also stipulated that Syrian forces were to remain in Lebanon for a period of up to two years, during which time they would assist the new government in establishing security arrangements. For his part, General Aoun was greatly opposed to the Ṭā'if Accord, fearing it

Mūsā al-Ṣadr

(b. 1928, Qom, Iran—disappeared August 31, 1978, Libya?)

Mūsā al-Ṣadr was an Iranian-born Lebanese Shīʿite cleric. The son of an ayatollah, he received a traditional Islamic education in Qom and in Al-Najaf, Iraq, and also briefly studied political economy and law at Tehrān University. In the late 1950s he moved to Lebanon, where he became involved in social work among the country's largely disfranchised Shīʿite community. In 1968–69 he formed the Higher Shīʿite Islamic Council to promote the community's interests, and in 1975 he formed Amal, an armed wing of his Ḥarakat al-Maḥrūmīn ("Movement of the Deprived"), a Shīʿite social reform movement, to defend the Shīʿite community in the Lebanese civil war. He and a small entourage disappeared while on an official trip in Libya. The Libyan government disavowed any knowledge of what became of the cleric and his companions. His disappearance remains a highly controversial mystery.

would provide a recipe for continued Syrian involvement in Lebanon.

Parliament subsequently convened on November 5, 1989, in Lebanon, where it ratified the Ṭā'if Accord and elected René Moawad to the presidency. Moawad was assassinated on November 22, and Elias Hrawi was elected two days later. However, General Aoun denounced both presidential elections as invalid. Several days later it was announced that General Aoun had again been dismissed from his position as head of the armed forces, and General Émile Lahoud was named in his place.

In January 1990 intense strife broke out in East Beirut between Aoun and Samir Geagea, who then headed the LF, which proved quite costly for the Maronite community and, over several months, resulted in the deaths of numerous (mostly Christian) Lebanese. The final vestiges of the Lebanese civil war were at last extinguished on October 13, 1990, when Syrian troops launched a ground and air attack against Aoun and forced him into exile. Throughout the war's duration, more than 100,000 people had been killed, nearly 1,000,000 displaced, and several billion dollars' worth of damage to property and infrastructure sustained.

Lebanon's Second Republic (1990–)

With the end of the civil war, it was left to the newly unified government of President Hrawi to embark upon the delicate and dangerous process of consolidating and extending the power of the Lebanese government. A new cabinet composed of many former militia leaders was appointed, and considerable effort was devoted to the demobilization of most of the wartime militias. The process of rebuilding the Lebanese army was begun under the auspices of General Lahoud, its new commander in

Hezbollah

Hezbollah (Arabic: Ḥizb Allāh ["Party of God"]) is a militia group and political party that first emerged as a faction in Lebanon following the Israeli invasion of that country in 1982.

Shīʿite Muslims, traditionally the weakest religious group in Lebanon, first found their voice in the moderate and largely secular Amal movement. Following the Islamic Revolution in Shīʿite Iran in 1979 and the Israeli invasion of Lebanon in 1982, a group of Lebanese Shīʿite clerics formed Hezbollah with the goal of driving Israel from Lebanon and establishing an Islamic state there. Hezbollah was based in the predominately Shīʿite areas of the Bekaa Valley, southern Lebanon, and southern Beirut. It coordinated its efforts closely with Iran, from which it acquired substantial logistical support, and drew its manpower largely from disaffected younger, more radical members of Amal. Throughout the 1980s Hezbollah engaged in increasingly sophisticated attacks against Israel and fought in Lebanon's civil war (1975–90), repeatedly coming to blows with Amal. During this time, Hezbollah allegedly engaged in terrorist attacks including kidnappings and car bombings, directed predominantly against Westerners, but also established a comprehensive social services network for its supporters.

Hezbollah was one of the few militia groups not disarmed by the Syrians at the end of the civil war, and they continued to fight a sustained guerrilla campaign against Israel in southern Lebanon until Israel's withdrawal in 2000. Hezbollah emerged as a leading political party in post–civil war Lebanon.

On July 12, 2006, Hezbollah, in an attempt to pressure Israel into releasing three Lebanese jailed in Israeli prisons, launched a military operation against Israel, killing a number of Israeli soldiers and abducting two as prisoners of war. This action led Israel to launch a major military offensive against Hezbollah. The 34-day war between Hezbollah and Israel resulted in the deaths of more than 1,000 Lebanese and the displacement of some 1,000,000. Fighting the Israeli Defense Forces to a standstill—a feat no other Arab militia had accomplished—Hezbollah and its leader, Hassan Nasrallah, emerged as heroes throughout much of the Arab world. In the months following the war, Hezbollah used its prestige to attempt to topple Lebanon's government after its demands for more cabinet seats were not met: its members, along with those of the Amal militia, resigned from the cabinet. The opposition then declared that the remaining cabinet had lost its legitimacy and demanded the formation of a new government in which Hezbollah and its opposition allies would possess the power of veto.

Late the following year, efforts by the National Assembly to select a successor at the end of Lebanese president Émile Lahoud's nine-year term were stalemated by the continued power struggle between the Hezbollah-led opposition and the Western-backed government. A boycott by the opposition—which continued to seek the veto power it had been denied—prevented the assembly from reaching a two-thirds quorum. Lahoud's term expired in November 2007, and the presidency remained unoccupied as the factions struggled to reach a consensus on a candidate and the makeup of the new government.

In May 2008, clashes between Hezbollah forces and government supporters in Beirut were sparked by government decisions that included plans to dismantle Hezbollah's private telecommunications network. Nasrallah equated the government decisions with a declaration of war and mobilized Hezbollah forces, which quickly took control of parts of Beirut. In the following days the government reversed the decisions that had sparked the outbreak of violence, and a summit attended by both factions in Qatar led to an agreement granting the Hezbollah-led opposition the veto power it had long sought.

In July 2008 Hezbollah and Israel concluded an agreement securing the exchange of several Lebanese prisoners and the remains of Lebanese and Palestinian fighters in return for the remains of Israeli soldiers, including the bodies of two soldiers whose capture by Hezbollah had sparked the brief war two years earlier.

chief. At tremendous cost and after more than 15 years, the Lebanese civil war was ended, and the framework for Lebanon's Second Republic had been established.

Politics and Reconstruction in Post–Civil War Lebanon

The destruction wrought by the country's massive civil war necessitated a sweeping program of reconstruction, which was largely undertaken by Prime Minister Rafiq al-Hariri following his appointment to the post after the 1992 parliamentary elections. Hariri's reconstruction plan, designed to revive the economy and reestablish Lebanon as a financial and commercial centre in the region, achieved the initial stabilization of the value of the Lebanese pound and succeeded in raising significant foreign capital on European bond markets, albeit at high rates of return.

The immediate challenges of Lebanon's post–civil war period were to institutionalize the political reforms agreed to at Ṭā'if and to reconstruct the country's social and economic infrastructure. Lebanon achieved important political successes with the transition of the presidency in 1998 from Hrawi to Lahoud, paralleled by the transition from Hariri's government to that of Salim al-Hoss that same year, and with the increasing legitimacy of the National Assembly in the Lebanese political process. The gradual reintegration of previously marginalized groups, facilitated by acceptance of the Ṭā'if reforms, meant an increased role for both the Maronite Christians (who had initially boycotted the electoral process) and Hezbollah, which became politically active in postwar Lebanon.

Continuing Challenges into the 21st Century: External Intervention and Confessional Conflict

The development of the Second Republic remained closely linked to its larger external environment—in particular, to Israel and Syria, the two principal players in Lebanon. Israel continued to exercise influence in its self-declared security zone in southern Lebanon, where it waged an ongoing war of attrition with Hezbollah's militia forces throughout the 1990s. However, in light of the increasingly costly war, Israeli support for a unilateral withdrawal from Lebanon had gathered significant momentum by the end of the decade, and Israeli troops were withdrawn in 2000. Hostility between Israel and Hezbollah, marked by periodic clashes and retaliatory exchanges of violence, continued into the early years of the 21st century. Tensions flared in July 2006, when Hezbollah launched an armed operation against Israel from southern Lebanon, killing a number of Israeli soldiers and abducting two as prisoners of war. This led Israel to launch a major military offensive against Hezbollah. The 34-day war between Hezbollah and Israel, in which more than 1,000 Lebanese and about 160 Israelis were killed and some 1,000,000 Lebanese were displaced, caused fresh damage to key services and infrastructure in southern Lebanon.

Meanwhile, following the agreement reached at Ṭāʾif, Syria also continued to exercise an extensive influence in Lebanon. Socioeconomic ties between Syria and Lebanon were facilitated by a series of bilateral treaties and agreements concluded between the two governments, the scope of which ranged from economic and trade ties to cultural and educational exchanges. On May 22, 1991, a treaty of "fraternity, coordination, and cooperation," interpreted by some as a legitimation of Syria's continued presence in Lebanon, was signed with Syria, and a defense and security pact followed. In addition, in spite of stipulations in the Ṭāʾif Accord that called for a withdrawal of Syrian troops to the Bekaa Valley by the end of 1992, Syria maintained a contingent of some 30,000 troops in Lebanon in the 1990s. With the Israeli withdrawal from the south of the country in 2000, however, calls for Syrian disengagement increased. Over the next several years, Syrian troops undertook a series of phased withdrawals and redeployments, gradually restructuring the number and distribution of Syria's armed forces in Lebanon. Overall troop strength for the Syrian army in Lebanon was reduced to about 14,000, but it was not until the assassination of Hariri in early 2005 that real domestic pressure for a full Syrian withdrawal began to grow. It was widely suspected that Hariri, who was then out of office, was killed at the behest of the Syrian government. The result was that hundreds of thousands of Lebanese—both against and for the Syrian presence—poured into the streets in a series of spontaneous mass protests. The last Syrian troops left Lebanon by mid-2005, and in late 2008 Syria and Lebanon established formal diplomatic ties for the first time.

While the Ṭāʾif Accord had called for a gradual end to confessionalism within the country, the reality in post–civil war Lebanon tended toward an entrenchment and strengthening of sectarian allegiances. The civil war resulted in the virtual elimination of multiconfessional regions where coexistence was the norm. As a result, sectarianism became increasingly geographically as well as culturally defined. Moreover, the electoral system continued to militate against the emergence of cross-cutting political parties with the ability to challenge the regional power bases of Lebanon's traditional *zuʿamāʾ*. In spite of the increased dynamism of the Lebanese parliament, real political power in Lebanon's Second Republic lay with the troika of sectarian leaders that occupied the offices of president, prime minister, and the speaker of the Assembly. Following the disarmament of the various militias of the civil war era, communal conflict was largely transplanted into the political arena, as political decisions largely became a result of elite confessional bargaining rather than an outcome of democratic process. Political divisions were further deepened by the fracture of the political process following the assassination of Hariri and the withdrawal of Syria from the country in 2005.

As the end of President Lahoud's nine-year period in office approached in late 2007, the Lebanese political process faced a stalemate. The National Assembly's attempt to select a successor was suspended in deadlock by a boycott led by the pro-Syrian opposition, which sought a greater share of political power and prevented the Assembly from achieving the necessary two-thirds quorum. As a result, Lahoud's term expired in November 2007 with no successor named. The post remained unoccupied as the opposing factions struggled to reach a consensus on a candidate and on the makeup of the new government.

As the political crisis drew on, clashes between Hezbollah forces and government supporters—sparked by government decisions that included plans to shut down Hezbollah's private telecommunications network—erupted in Beirut in May 2008. Hezbollah leader Hassan Nasrallah equated these moves with a declaration of war and mobilized Hezbollah forces, which swiftly took control of parts of the city. In the following days the government reversed the decisions that had sparked the outbreak of violence, and a summit attended by both factions in Qatar led to an agreement granting the Hezbollah-led opposition the veto power it had long sought.

On May 25, 2008, General Michel Suleiman was elected president, ending months of political impasse. He reappointed Fuad Siniora, who had been prime minister since mid-2005, at the head of a new unity government soon thereafter, and, after several weeks of negotiation, the makeup of the new government was agreed upon. Reconciliation efforts continued, and in October 2008 a new election law that restructured voting districts was passed. That same month Lebanon and Syria established diplomatic relations for the first time in both countries' independent histories.

Although Lebanon experienced relative stability following the Qatar-mediated agreement, tensions escalated with the approach of parliamentary elections scheduled for June 2009. Voter turnout in the election reached

Hassan Nasrallah

(b. August 31, 1960, Beirut, Lebanon)

Hassan Abdel Karim Nasrallah is a Lebanese militia and political leader who has served as leader (secretary-general) of Hezbollah since 1992.

Nasrallah was raised in the impoverished Karantina district of eastern Beirut, where his father ran a small grocery store. As a boy Nasrallah was an earnest student of Islam. After the outbreak of civil war in Lebanon in 1975 caused the family to flee south from Beirut, Nasrallah joined Amal, a Lebanese Shīʿite paramilitary group with ties to Iran and Syria. Soon afterward he left for Najaf, Iraq, to study at the Shīʿite seminary there. Following the expulsion of hundreds of Lebanese students from Iraq in 1978, he returned to Lebanon and fought with Amal, becoming the group's Bekaa Valley commander. Following Israel's invasion of Lebanon in 1982, Nasrallah left Amal to join the nascent Hezbollah movement, a more-radical force that was heavily influenced by Ayatollah Ruhollah Khomeini and the 1979 Islamic Revolution in Iran.

Nasrallah rose through Hezbollah's ranks, and in 1988, when tensions with Amal flared, Nasrallah fought on the front lines. He assumed leadership of Hezbollah in 1992 after his predecessor, Sheikh ʿAbbas al-Musawi, was killed by an Israeli missile. As a leader and cleric, Nasrallah relied on charisma and subtle charm to express his message. He was not a fiery or intimidating speaker. Rather, he came across as thoughtful, humble, and at times humorous. He emphasized the importance of Arab dignity and honour.

Under Nasrallah, Hezbollah staged attacks on Israeli forces occupying southern Lebanon until Israel withdrew in 2000. Nasrallah was not unscathed in the effort. In 1997 his 18-year-old son, Hadi, was killed while fighting Israeli forces. Nasrallah was also credited with arranging a prisoner exchange with Israel in 2004 that many Arabs considered a victory.

In July 2006, in an effort to pressure Israel into releasing three Lebanese jailed in Israeli prisons, Hezbollah paramilitary forces launched a military operation from the south, killing a number of Israeli soldiers and abducting two. This action led Israel to launch a major military offensive against Hezbollah. At the beginning of the war, some Arab leaders criticized Nasrallah and Hezbollah for inciting the conflict. But by the end of the 34-day war, which resulted in the deaths of more than 1,000 Lebanese and the displacement of some one million others, Nasrallah had declared victory and had emerged as a revered leader in much of the Arab world, as Hezbollah was able to fight the Israeli Defense Forces to a standstill—a feat that no other Arab militia had accomplished.

its highest point since the civil war period, and the pro-Western March 14 bloc—named for the date in 2005 on which thousands gathered to protest Syrian military presence in Lebanon—emerged from the contest having maintained its majority. Voting was considered generally free and fair, although international observers expressed concern at some tactics, including vote buying, that took place in the preelection period.

Shortly after the March 14 bloc's electoral victory, its leader—Saad al-Hariri, the son of former prime minister Rafiq al-Hariri—was named prime minister and charged by President Suleiman with the complex task of forming a unity government. Weeks of negotiations with the opposition proved fruitless, however, and after more than two months Hariri announced that he would abandon attempts to form the government and would step down as prime minister–designate. The following week, however, President Suleiman once more designated Hariri prime minister and asked that he try again to form the government. Hariri continued his efforts, and in early November, following months of negotiations, he announced that a unity government had been successfully formed. The cabinet included 15 seats allotted to Hariri's majority, 10 seats for Hezbollah, and 5 seats for candidates nominated by President Suleiman.

CHAPTER 11

Jordan: The Land and Its People

Jordan, situated in the rocky desert of the northern Arabian Peninsula, is a young state in an ancient land. It is bounded to the north by Syria, to the east by Iraq, to the southeast and south by Saudi Arabia, and to the west by Israel and the West Bank. The West Bank area (so named because it lies just west of the Jordan River) was under Jordanian rule from 1948 to 1967, but in 1988 Jordan renounced its claims to the area. Jordan has 16 miles (26 km) of coastline on the Gulf of Aqaba in the southwest, where Al-'Aqabah, its only port, is located.

Arabs account for the majority of the population of Jordan. These are mainly Jordanians and Palestinians.

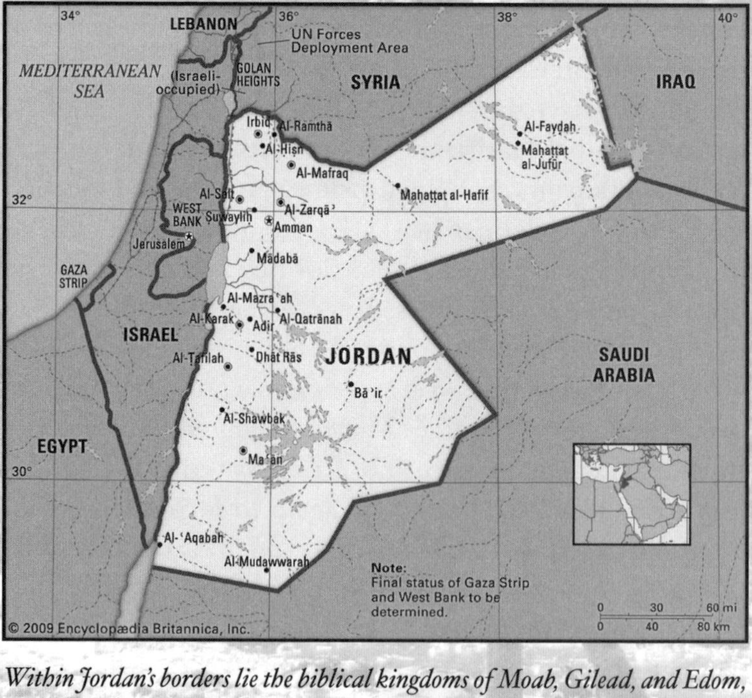

Within Jordan's borders lie the biblical kingdoms of Moab, Gilead, and Edom, as well as the renowned red stone city of Petra.

Bedouins form a substantial minority and were the largest indigenous group before the influx of Palestinians in the mid-20th century. Jordan is the only Arab country to have granted citizenship to its Palestinian population on such a large scale.

RELIEF

Jordan has three major physiographic regions (from east to west): the desert, the uplands east of the Jordan River, and the Jordan Valley (the northwest portion of the great East African Rift System).

The desert region is mostly within the Syrian Desert—an extension of the Arabian Desert—and occupies the eastern and southern parts of the country, comprising more than four-fifths of its territory. The desert's northern part is composed of volcanic lava and basalt, and its southern part of outcrops of sandstone and granite. The landscape is much eroded, primarily by wind. The uplands east of the Jordan River, an escarpment overlooking the rift valley, have an average elevation of 2,000–3,000 feet (600–900 m) and rise to about 5,755 feet (1,754 m) at Mount Ramm, Jordan's highest point, in the south. Outcrops of sandstone, chalk, limestone, and flint extend to the extreme south, where igneous rocks predominate.

The Jordan Valley drops to an average of 1,312 feet (400 m) below sea level at the Dead Sea, the lowest natural point on the Earth's surface.

DRAINAGE

The Jordan River, approximately 186 miles (300 km) in length, meanders south, draining the waters of Lake Tiberias (better known as the Sea of Galilee), the Yarmūk

Dead Sea

The Dead Sea (Arabic: Al-Baḥr al-Mayyit; Hebrew: Yam HaMelaẖ; also known as the Salt Sea) is a landlocked salt lake between Israel and Jordan, which lies some 1,300 feet (400 m) below sea level—the lowest elevation and the lowest body of water on the surface of the Earth. Its eastern shore belongs to Jordan, and the southern half of its western shore belongs to Israel. The northern half of the western shore lies within the West Bank and has been under Israeli occupation since the June (Six-Day) War of 1967. Because of its location, navigation on the Dead Sea is negligible. Its shores are nearly deserted, and permanent establishments are rare.

The Jordan River flows from the north into the Dead Sea, which is 50 miles (80 km) long and attains a width of 11 miles (18 km). The peninsula of Al-Lisān (Arabic meaning "The Tongue") divides the lake on its eastern side into two unequal basins: the northern basin encompasses about three-fourths of the lake's total surface area and reaches

Salt deposits on the southwestern shore of the Dead Sea near Masada, Israel. Z. Radovan, Jerusalem

a depth of 1,300 feet (400 m). The southern basin is smaller and shallower (less than 10 feet [3 m] on average).

The waters of the Dead Sea are extremely saline, and the concentration of salt increases toward the bottom. The deep water is fossilized (i.e., being exceptionally salty and dense, it remains permanently on the bottom). The near-surface water dates from a few centuries after biblical times. The saline water has a high density that keeps bathers buoyant. The fresh water of the Jordan stays on the surface, and in the spring its muddy colour can be traced across the lake as far as 30 miles (50 km) south of the point where the river empties into the Dead Sea. The lake's extreme salinity excludes all forms of life except bacteria. Fish carried in by the Jordan or by smaller streams when in flood die quickly. Apart from the vegetation along the rivers, plant life along the shores is discontinuous and consists mainly of halophytes (salt-tolerant plants).

River, and the valley streams of both plateaus into the Dead Sea, which occupies the central area of the valley. The soil of its lower reaches is highly saline, and the shores of the Dead Sea consist of salt marshes inhospitable to vegetation. To its south, Wadi Al-'Arabah (also called Wadi Al-Jayb), a completely desolate region, is thought to contain mineral resources.

In the northern uplands several valleys containing perennial streams run west. Around Al-Karak they flow west, east, and north. South of Al-Karak intermittent valley streams run east toward Al-Jafr Depression.

SOILS

The country's best soils are found in the Jordan Valley and in the area southeast of the Dead Sea. The topsoil in both regions consists of alluvium—deposited by the Jordan

River and washed from the uplands, respectively—with the soil in the valley generally being deposited in fans spread over various grades of marl.

CLIMATE

Jordan's climate varies from Mediterranean in the west to desert in the east and south, but the land is generally arid. The proximity of the Mediterranean Sea is the major influence on climates, although continental air masses and elevation also modify it. Average monthly temperatures at Amman in the north range from the mid-40s to the high 70s °F (low 10s to mid-20s °C), while at Al-'Aqabah in the far south they range from the low 60s to the low 90s °F (mid-10s to low 30s °C). The prevailing winds throughout the country are westerly to southwesterly, but spells of hot, dry, dusty winds blowing from the southeast off the Arabian Peninsula frequently occur and bring the country its most uncomfortable weather. Known locally as the khamsin, these winds blow most often in the early and late summer and can last for several days at a time before terminating abruptly as the wind direction changes and much cooler air follows.

Precipitation occurs in the short, cool winters, decreasing from 16 inches (400 mm) annually in the northwest near the Jordan River to less than 4 inches (100 mm) in the south. In the uplands east of the Jordan River, the annual total is about 14 inches (355 mm). The valley itself has a yearly average of 8 inches (200 mm), and the desert regions receive one-fourth of that. Occasional snow and frost occur in the uplands but are rare in the rift valley. As the population increases, water shortages in the major towns are becoming one of Jordan's crucial problems.

PLANT AND ANIMAL LIFE

The flora of Jordan falls into three distinct types: Mediterranean, steppe (treeless plains), and desert. In the uplands the Mediterranean type predominates with scrubby, dense bushes and small trees, while in the drier steppe region to the east species of the genus *Artemisia* (wormwood) are most frequent. Grasses are the prevalent vegetation on the steppe, but isolated trees and shrubs, such as lotus fruit and the Mount Atlas pistachio, also occur. In the desert, vegetation grows meagrely in depressions and on the sides and floors of the valleys after the scant winter rains.

Only a tiny portion of Jordan's area is forested, most of it occurring in the rocky highlands. These forests have survived the depredations of villagers and nomads alike. The Jordanian government promotes reforestation by providing free seedlings to farmers. In the higher regions of the uplands, the predominant types of trees are the Aleppo oak (*Quercus infectoria Olivier*), the kermes oak (*Quercus coccinea*), the Palestinian pistachio (*Pistacia palaestina*), the Aleppo pine (*Pinus halepensis*), and the eastern strawberry tree (*Arbutus andrachne*). Wild olives also are found there, and the Phoenician juniper (*Juniperus phoenicea L.*) occurs in the regions with lower precipitation levels. The national flower is the black iris (*Iris nigricans*).

The varied wildlife includes wild boars, ibex, and a species of wild goat found in the gorges and in the ʿAyn al-Azraq oasis. Hares, jackals, foxes, wildcats, hyenas, wolves, gazelles, blind mole rats, mongooses, and a few leopards also inhabit the area. Centipedes, scorpions, and various types of lizards are found as well. Birds include the golden eagle and the vulture, while wild fowl include the pigeon and the partridge.

ETHNIC GROUPS

The overwhelming majority of the people are Arabs, principally Jordanians and Palestinians. There is also a significant minority of Bedouin, who were by far the largest indigenous group before the influx of Palestinians following the Arab-Israeli wars of 1948–49 and 1967. Jordanians of Bedouin heritage remain committed to the Hāshimite regime, which has ruled the country since 1923, in spite of having become a minority there. Although the Palestinian population is often critical of the monarchy, Jordan is the only Arab country to grant wide-scale citizenship to Palestinian refugees. Other minorities include a number of Iraqis who fled to Jordan as a result of the Persian Gulf War and Iraq War. There are also smaller Circassian (known locally as Cherkess or Jarkas) and Armenian communities. A small number of Turkmen (who speak either an ancient form of the Turkmen language or the Azeri language) also reside in Jordan.

The indigenous Arabs, whether Muslim or Christian, used to trace their ancestry from the northern Arabian Qaysī (Maʿddī, Nizārī, ʿAdnānī, or Ismāʿīlī) tribes or from the southern Arabian Yamanī (Banū Kalb or Qaḥṭānī) groups. Only a few tribes and towns have continued to observe this Qaysī-Yamanī division—a pre-Islamic split that was once an important, although broad, source of social identity as well as a point of social friction and conflict.

LANGUAGES

Nearly all the people speak Arabic, the country's official language. There are various dialects spoken, with local inflections and accents, but these are mutually intelligible and similar to the type of Levantine Arabic spoken in parts of Palestine, Lebanon, and Syria. There is, as in all parts of the Arab world, a significant difference between the written language—known as Modern Standard Arabic—and the colloquial, spoken form. The former is similar to Classical Arabic and is taught in school. Most Circassians have adopted Arabic in daily life, though some continue to speak Adyghe (one of the Caucasian languages). Armenian is also spoken in pockets, but bilingualism or outright assimilation to the Arabic language is common among all minorities.

RELIGION

Virtually the entire population is Sunni Muslim. Christians constitute most of the rest, of whom two-thirds adhere to the Greek Orthodox Church. Other Christian groups include the Greek Catholics, also called the Melchites, or Catholics of the Byzantine rite, who recognize the supremacy of the Roman pope; the Roman Catholic community, headed by a pope-appointed patriarch; and the small Syrian Orthodox Patriarchate of Antioch, or Syrian Jacobite Church, whose members use Syriac in their liturgy. Most non-Arab Christians are Armenians, and the majority belong to the Gregorian, or Armenian, Orthodox church, while the rest attend the Armenian Catholic Church. There are several Protestant denominations representing communities whose converts came almost entirely from other Christian sects.

The Druze, an offshoot of the Ismāʿīlī Shīʿite sect, number a few hundred and reside in and around Amman. About 1,000 Bahāʾī—who in the 19th century also split off from Shīʿite Islam—live in Al-ʿAdasiyyah in the Jordan Valley. The Armenians, Druze, and Bahāʾī are both religious and ethnic communities. The Circassians are mostly

Sunni, and they, along with the closely related Chechens (Shīshān)—a Shī'ite group, numbering about 1,000, who are descendants of 19th-century immigrants from the Caucasus Mountains—make up the most important non-Arab minority.

SETTLEMENT PATTERNS

The landscape falls into two regions—the desert zone and the cultivated zone—each of which is associated with its own mode of living. The tent-dwelling nomads (Bedouin, or Badū), who make up some one-tenth of the population, generally inhabit the desert, some areas of the steppe, and the uplands. The tent-dwelling Bedouin people have decreased in number because the government has successfully enforced their permanent settlement. Urban residents who trace their roots to the Bedouin make up more than one-third of Jordanians.

The eastern Bedouin are principally camel breeders and herders, while the western Bedouin herd sheep and goats. There are some seminomads, in whom the modes of life of the desert and the cultivated zones merge. These people adopt a nomadic existence during part of the year but return to their lands and homes in time to practice agriculture. The two largest nomadic groups of Jordan are the Banū (Banī) Ṣakhr and Banū al-Ḥuwayṭāt. The grazing grounds of both are entirely within Jordan, as is the case with the smaller tribe of Sirḥān. There are numerous lesser groups, such as the Banū Ḥasan and Banū Khālid as well as the Hawazim, 'Aṭiyyah, and Sharafāt. These traditionally paid protection money to larger groups. The Ruwālah (Rwala) tribe, which is not indigenous, passes through Jordan in its yearly migration from Syria to Saudi Arabia.

Rural residents, including small numbers of Bedouin, constitute about one-sixth of the population. The average

Roman theatre ruins (foreground)*, surrounded by the city of Amman, Jordan.* Ara Guler, Istanbul

village contains a cluster of houses and other buildings, including an elementary school and a mosque, with pasturage on the outskirts. A medical dispensary and a post office may be found in the larger villages, together with a general store and a small café, whose owners are usually part-time farmers. Kinship relationships are patriarchal, while extended-family ties govern social relationships and tribal organization.

More than four-fifths of all Jordanians live in urban areas. The main population centres are Amman, Al-Zarqāʾ, Irbid, and Al-Ruṣayfah. Many of the smaller towns have only a few thousand inhabitants. Most towns have hospitals, banks, government and private schools, mosques, churches, libraries, and entertainment facilities, and some have institutions of higher learning and newspapers. Amman and Al-Zarqāʾ, and to some extent Irbid, have more modern urban characteristics than do the smaller towns.

DEMOGRAPHIC TRENDS

The population of Jordan is predominantly young. Persons younger than age 15 constitute almost two-fifths of the population, and some two-thirds of the population is younger than age 30. The birth rate is high, and the country's population growth rate is about double the world average. The average life expectancy is also higher than the world average. Internal migration from rural to urban centres has added a burden to the economy, however, many Jordanians live and work abroad.

Some one-third of Jordan's population are Palestinians. The influx of Palestinian refugees not only altered Jordan's demographic map but has also affected its political, social, and economic life. Jordan's population in the late 1940s

Irbid

Irbid is a city in northern Jordan. It was built on successive Early Bronze Age settlements and was possibly the biblical Beth Arbel and the Arbila of the Decapolis, a Hellenistic league of the 1st century BCE through the 2nd century CE. The population of Irbid swelled in the late 19th century, and prior to 1948 it served as a significant centre of transit trade.

Modern Irbid is one of Jordan's industrial areas as well as an agricultural centre for Jordan's most fertile region. The many springs in the area, in addition to the Yarmūk River, provide water for the irrigation of crops. Yarmūk University (1976) offers instruction in both Arabic and English, with numerous faculties in the arts and sciences, education, law, and engineering. Jordan University of Science and Technology (1986) is also located in Irbid.

was between 200,000 and 250,000. After the 1948–49 Arab-Israeli war and the annexation of the West Bank, Jordanian citizenship was granted to some 400,000 Palestinians who were residents of and remained in the West Bank and to about half a million refugees from the new Israeli state. Many refugees settled east of the Jordan River. Between 1949 and 1967, Palestinians continued to move east in large numbers. After the 1967 war, an estimated 310,000 to 350,000 Palestinians, mostly from the West Bank, sought refuge in Jordan. Thereafter immigration from the West Bank continued at a lower rate. During the Persian Gulf War (1990–91), some 300,000 additional Palestinians fled (or were expelled) from Kuwait to Jordan, and as many as 1.7 million Iraqis flooded into the kingdom during the war and the years that followed. Another smaller wave arrived in 2003 after the start of the

Iraq War. Most of these Iraqis left, but perhaps 200,000 to 300,000 remain. Only a small fraction are registered as refugees.

Most Palestinians are employed and hold full Jordanian citizenship. By the early 21st century, approximately 1.6 million Palestinians were registered with the United Nations Relief and Works Agency for Palestine Refugees in the Near East (UNRWA), an organization providing education, medical care, relief assistance, and social services. About one-sixth of these refugees lived in camps in Jordan.

CHAPTER 12

The Jordanian Economy

Although Jordan's economy is relatively small and faces numerous obstacles, it is comparatively well diversified. Services account for two-thirds of Jordan's gross domestic product (GDP). Remittances from Jordanians working abroad are a major source of foreign exchange.

Jordan has increasingly been plagued by recession, debt, and unemployment since the mid-1990s. The small size of the Jordanian market, fluctuations in agricultural production, a lack of capital, and the presence of large numbers of refugees have made it necessary for Jordan to continue to seek foreign aid. The Jordanian government has been slow to implement privatization. In spite of efforts by the International Monetary Fund (IMF) and the World Bank to boost the private sector—including agreements to write off the country's external debt and loans from the World Bank designed to revitalize Jordan's economy—it was only in 1999 that the government began introducing a number of economic reforms. These efforts included Jordan's entry into the World Trade Organization (in 2000) and the partial privatization of some state-owned enterprises.

Perhaps most important, Jordan's geographic location has made it and its economy highly vulnerable to political instability in the region. The Jordanian economy was resilient and growing before the June (Six-Day) War of 1967, and the West Bank, prior to its occupation by Israel during that conflict, contributed about one-third of Jordan's total domestic income. Economic growth continued after 1967 at a slower pace but was revitalized by a series of state economic plans. Trade increased between Jordan and Iraq during the Iran-Iraq War (1980–88), because Iraq required access to Jordan's port of Al-'Aqabah. Jordan initially supported Iraqi president Ṣaddām Ḥussein when Iraq occupied Kuwait during the Persian Gulf War, but it eventually agreed to United Nations (UN) trade sanctions against Iraq, its principal trading partner, and thereby put its whole economy in jeopardy. External emergency aid helped Jordan weather the crisis, and the economy was boosted by the sudden influx of Palestinians from Kuwait in 1991, many of whom brought in capital. During 2003 the construction industry recovered with the arrival of many thousands of people fleeing Iraq, and Jordan became a major service centre for those working to reconstruct that country. In spite of the support of the government for IMF and World Bank plans to increase the private sector, the state remains the dominant force in Jordan's economy.

AGRICULTURE

Only a tiny fraction of Jordan's land is arable, and the country imports some foodstuffs to meet its needs. Wheat and barley are the main crops of the rain-fed uplands, and irrigated land in the Jordan Valley produces citrus and other fruits, potatoes, tomatoes, cucumbers, and olives. Pastureland is limited. Although artesian wells have been dug to increase its area, much former pasture area has been turned over to the cultivation of olive and fruit trees, and large areas have been degraded to the point that they can barely support livestock. Sheep and goats are the most important livestock, but there are also some cattle, camels, horses, donkeys, and mules. Poultry is also kept.

RESOURCES AND POWER

Mineral resources include large deposits of phosphates, potash, limestone, and marble, as well as dolomite, kaolin, and salt. More recently discovered minerals include barite

Although little land is available for livestock, goats are valuable enough to warrant the grazing space. Sylvester Adams/Digital Vision/Getty Images

(the principal ore of the metallic element barium), quartzite, gypsum (used as a fertilizer), and feldspar, and there are unexploited deposits of copper, uranium, and shale oil. Although the country has no significant oil deposits, modest reserves of natural gas are located in its eastern desert. In 2003 the first section of a new pipeline from Egypt began delivering natural gas to Al-ʿAqabah.

Virtually all electric power in Jordan is generated by thermal plants, most of which are oil-fired. The major power stations are linked by a transmission system. By the early 21st century, the government had completed a program to link the major cities and towns by a countrywide grid.

Beginning in the final decades of the 20th century, access to water became a major problem for Jordan—as well as a point of conflict among states in the region—as overuse of the Jordan River (and its tributary, the Yarmūk River) and excessive tapping of the region's natural aquifers led to shortages throughout Jordan and surrounding countries. In 2000 Jordan and Syria secured funding for constructing a dam on the Yarmūk River that, in addition to storing water for Jordan, would also generate electricity for Syria. Construction of the Waḥdah ("Unity") Dam began in 2004.

MANUFACTURING

Manufacturing is concentrated around Amman. The extraction of phosphate, petroleum refining, and cement production are the country's major heavy industries. Food, clothing, and a variety of consumer goods also are produced.

FINANCE

The Central Bank of Jordan (Al-Bank al-Markazī al-Urdunī) issues the dinar, the national currency. There are many national and foreign banks in addition to credit institutions. The government has participated with private enterprise in establishing the largest mining, industrial, and tourist firms in the country and also owns a significant share of the largest companies. The Amman Stock Exchange (Būrṣat 'Ammān; formerly the Amman Financial Market) is one of the largest stock markets in the Arab world.

TRADE

Jordan's primary exports are clothing, chemicals and chemical products, and potash and phosphates. The main imports are mineral products, machinery and apparatus, and food products. Major trading partners include Saudi Arabia, the United States, and regional neighbours. In 2000 Jordan signed a bilateral free trade agreement with the United States. The value of exports has been growing, but it does not cover that of imports. The deficit is financed by foreign grants, loans, and other forms of capital transfers. Although Jordan's trade deficit has been large, it has been offset somewhat by revenue from tourism, remittances sent by Jordanians working abroad, earnings from foreign investments made by the central bank, and subsidies from other Arab and non-Arab governments.

SERVICES

Services, including public administration, defense, and retail sales, form the single most important component of Jordan's economy in both value and employment. The country's vulnerable geography has led to high military expenditures, which are well above the world average.

The Jordanian government vigorously promotes tourism, and the number of tourists visiting Jordan has grown dramatically since the mid-1990s. Visitors mainly come from the West to see the old biblical cities of the Jordan Valley and such wonders as the ancient city of Petra, designated a World Heritage site in 1985. Income from tourism, mostly consisting of foreign reserves, has become a major factor in Jordan's efforts to reduce its balance-of-payments deficit.

LABOUR AND TAXATION

Jordan has also lost much of its skilled labour to neighbouring countries—as many as 400,000 people left the

King's Highway

The King's Highway (also known as the Via Nova Traiana) is an ancient thoroughfare that connected Syria and the Gulf of Aqaba by way of what is now Jordan. Mentioned in the Old Testament, it is one of the world's oldest continuously used communication routes.

The King's Highway was an important thoroughfare for north-south trade from ancient times. The Roman emperor Trajan (ruled 98–117 CE) renovated the road to improve transportation and communications between the regional capital, Bostra, and Al-'Aqabah. The renovated road was known specifically as the Via Nova Traiana to distinguish it from another road that Trajan constructed, the Via Traiana in Italy. The King's Highway was also an important thoroughfare during the Crusades, and numerous fortified castles remain along its route.

The development of similar routes—including the Pilgrimage Route, and, later, the Hejaz Railway and the Desert Highway—largely eclipsed the King's Highway. Nevertheless, it is promoted as a tourist attraction and is a picturesque means of exploring parts of the Jordanian countryside. The road links some of Jordan's most important historical sites, including those at Mādabā, Al-Karak, Al-Ṭafīlah, Al-Shawbak, and Petra, and also traverses important natural sites, including Wadi Al-Mawjib, wherein lies the 124-square-mile (320-square-km) Ḍānā Biosphere Reserve.

country in the early 1980s—although the problem has eased somewhat. This change is a result both of better employment opportunities within Jordan itself and of a curb on foreign labour demands by the Persian Gulf states.

The majority of the workforce is men, with women constituting roughly one-fourth of the total. Labour unions and employer organizations are legal, but the trade-union movement is weak. This is partly offset by the government, which has its own procedures for settling labour disputes.

More than half of the government's revenue is derived from taxes. Even though the government has made a great effort to reform the income tax, both to increase revenue and to redistribute income, revenue from indirect taxes continues to exceed that from direct taxes. Tax measures have been adopted to increase the rate of savings necessary for financing investments, and the government has implemented tax exemptions on foreign investments and on the transfer of foreign profits and capital.

TRANSPORTATION AND TELECOMMUNICATIONS

Jordan has a main, secondary, and rural road network, most of which is hard-surfaced. This roadway system, maintained by the Ministry of Public Works and Housing, not only links the major cities and towns but also connects the kingdom with neighbouring countries. One of the main traffic arteries is the Amman–Jarash–Al-Ramthā highway, which links Jordan with Syria. The Desert Highway, the route from Amman via Maʿān to the port of Al-ʿAqabah, is the principal route to the sea. From Maʿān the Desert Highway passes through Al-Mudawwarah, linking Jordan with Saudi Arabia. The King's Highway, a thoroughfare that dates to ancient times, also reaches Al-ʿAqabah and is promoted as a scenic route. The Amman-Jerusalem highway, passing through Nāʿūr, is a major tourist artery. The government-operated Hejaz-Jordan Railway extends from Darʿā in the north via Amman to Maʿān in the south. The Aqaba Railway Corporation operates a southern line that runs to the port of Al-ʿAqabah and connects to the Hejaz-Jordan Railway at Baṭn al-Ghūl. Rail connections also join Darʿā in the north with Damascus, Syria.

Royal Jordanian is the country's official airline, offering worldwide service. Queen Alia International Airport near Al-Jīzah, south of Amman, opened in 1983. Amman and Al-ʿAqabah have smaller international airports.

In 1994 Jordan introduced a program to reform its telecommunication system. The government-owned Jordan Telecommunications Corporation, the sole service provider, had been unable to meet demand or provide adequate service, particularly in rural areas; it was privatized in 1997. Since then, the use of cellular telephones has mushroomed, far outstripping standard telephone use. In addition, Internet use has grown dramatically.

CHAPTER 13

Jordanian Government and Society

The 1952 constitution is the most recent of a series of legislative instruments that, both before and after independence, have increased executive responsibility. The constitution declares Jordan to be a constitutional, hereditary monarchy with a parliamentary form of government. Islam is the official religion, and Jordan is declared to be part of the Arab *ummah* ("nation"). The king remains the country's ultimate authority and wields power over the executive, legislative, and judicial branches. Jordan's central government is headed by a prime minister appointed by the king, who also chooses the cabinet. According to the constitution, the appointments of both prime minister and cabinet are subject to parliamentary approval. The cabinet coordinates the work of the different departments and establishes general policy.

Jordan's constitution provides for a bicameral National Assembly (Majlis al-Ummah), with a Senate (Majlis al-Aʿyan) as its upper chamber, and a House of Representatives (Majlis al-Nuwwāb) as its lower chamber. The *aʿyan* ("notables") of the Senate are appointed by the king for four-year terms. Elections for the *nuwwāb* ("deputies") of the House of Representatives, scheduled at least every four years, frequently have been suspended. The ninth parliament, elected in 1965, was prorogued several times before being replaced in 1978 by the National Consultative Council, an appointed body with reduced power that debates government programs and activities. The parliament was reconvened, however, in a special session called in January 1984. Since then the parliament has been periodically suspended: from 1988, when Jordan severed its ties with the West Bank, until 1989 and from August until November 1993, when the country held its first multiparty elections since 1956. In 2001 the king dissolved the Majlis al-Nuwwāb to reformulate the electoral system, and new deputies were elected in 2003.

LOCAL GOVERNMENT

Jordan is divided into *muḥāfaẓāt* (governorates), which in turn are divided into districts and subdistricts, each of which is headed by an official appointed by the minister of the interior. Cities and towns each have mayors and partially elected councils.

JUSTICE

The judiciary is constitutionally independent, though judges are appointed and dismissed by royal *irādah* ("decree") following a decision made by the Justices Council. There are three categories of courts. The first category consists of regular courts, including those of magistrates, courts of first instance, and courts of appeals and cassation in Amman, which hear appeals passed on from lower courts. The constitution also provides for the Diwān Khāṣṣ (Special Council), which interprets the laws and passes on their constitutionality. The second category consists of Sharīʿah courts and other religious courts for non-Muslims, which exercise jurisdiction over matters of personal status. The third category consists of special courts, such as land, government, property, municipal, tax, and customs courts.

POLITICAL PROCESS

Jordanians 18 years of age and older may vote. Political parties were banned before the elections in 1963, however. Between 1971 and 1976, when it was abolished, the Arab

National Union (originally called the Jordanian National Union) was the only political organization allowed. Although not a political party, the transnational Muslim Brotherhood continued, with the tacit approval of the government, to engage in socially active functions. And it captured more than one-fourth of the lower house in the 1989 election. In 1992 political parties were legalized—as long as they acknowledged the legitimacy of the monarchy. Since then, the brotherhood has maintained a significant minority presence in Jordanian politics through its political arm, the Islamic Action Front.

SECURITY

Although their political influence has now diminished, the Bedouin, traditionally a martial desert people, still form the core of Jordan's army and occupy key positions in the military. Participation in the military is optional, and males can enter service at age 17. The Jordanian armed forces include an army and an air force equipped with sophisticated jet aircraft, which developed from the Arab Legion. There is also a small navy that acts as a coast guard. The king is commander in chief of the armed forces.

HEALTH AND WELFARE

The country's infant mortality rate is well below the world average. Most infectious diseases have been brought under control, and the number of physicians per capita has grown rapidly. Comprehensive health facilities are operated by the government, but hospitals are found only in major urban centres. A national health insurance program covers medical, dental, and eye care at a modest cost. Service is provided free to the poor. Welfare services were private until the mid-1950s, when the government

Traditionally martial desert people, the Bedouin hold key positions in the military and make up much of the military itself. Salah Malkawi/ Getty Images

assumed responsibility. Besides supervising and coordinating social and charitable organizations, the ministry administers welfare programs.

HOUSING

The housing situation has remained critical in spite of continuing construction. Surveys conducted in Amman and the eastern Jordan Valley show that most households live in one-room dwellings. The Housing Corporation and the Jordan Valley Authority build units for low-income families, and urban renewal projects in Amman and Al-Zarqāʾ have provided new and renovated units. Housing outside of the cities and major towns remains austere, and a small number of Bedouin still live in their traditional black tents.

EDUCATION

The great majority of the population is literate, although literacy rates remain higher among men than among women. Jordan has three types of schools: government schools, private schools, and the UNRWA schools that have been set up for Palestinian refugee children. Schooling consists of six years of elementary, three years of preparatory, and three years of secondary education. The Ministry of Education supervises all schools and establishes the curricula, teachers' qualifications, and state examinations; distributes free books to students in government schools; and enforces compulsory education to the age of 14. Most students attend government schools. Jordan's oldest institutions of higher learning include the University of Jordan (1962), Yarmūk University (1976), and Mu'tah University (1981). Many new universities were established in the 1990s. In addition to Khadduri Agricultural Training Institute, there are agricultural secondary schools as well as a number of vocational, labour, and social affairs institutes, a Sharīʿah legal seminary, and nursing, military, and teachers colleges.

CHAPTER 14

Jordanian Cultural Life

Jordan is an integral part of the Arab world and thus shares a cultural tradition common to the region. The family is of central importance to Jordanian life. Although their numbers have fallen as many have settled and adopted urban culture, the rural Bedouin population still follows a more traditional way of life, preserving customs passed down for generations. Village life revolves around the extended family, agriculture, and hospitality, with modernity existing only in the form of a motorized vehicle for transportation. Urban-dwelling Jordanians, however, enjoy all aspects of modern, popular culture, from theatrical productions and musical concerts to operas and ballet performances. Most major towns have movie theatres that offer both Arab and foreign films. Younger Jordanians frequent Internet cafés in the capital, where espresso is served at computer terminals.

The country's cuisine features dishes using beans, olive oil, yogurt, and garlic. Jordan's two most popular dishes are *msakhan*, lamb or mutton and rice with a yogurt sauce, and *mansaf*, chicken cooked with onions, which are both served on holidays and on special family occasions. Daily fare includes *khubz* (flatbread) with vegetable dips, grilled meats, and stews, served with sweet tea or coffee flavoured with cardamom.

Holidays that are celebrated in the kingdom include the Prophet Muhammad's birthday, as well as ʿĪd al-Fiṭr ("Festival of the Breaking fast," marking the end of Ramadan), ʿĪd al-Aḍḥa ("Festival of the Sacrifice," marking the culmination of the annual pilgrimage to Mecca), and other major Islamic festivals. Holidays observed by Jordan's small Christian minority include Palm Sunday, Easter, and

Christmas Day. Secular events include Independence Day and the birthday of the late King Ḥussein.

THE ARTS

Both private and governmental efforts have been made to foster the arts through various cultural centres, notably in Amman and Irbid, and through the establishment of art and cultural festivals throughout the country. Modernity has weakened the traditional Islamic injunction against the depiction of images of humans and animals. Thus, in addition to traditional architecture, decorative design, and various handicrafts, it is possible to find non-utilitarian forms of both representational and abstract painting and sculpture. Elaborate calligraphy and geometric designs often enhance manuscripts and mosques. As in the rest of the region, the oral tradition is prominent in literary expression. Jordan's most famous poet, Muṣṭafā Wahbah al-Ṭāl, ranks among the major Arab poets of the 20th century. After World War II a number of important poets and prose writers emerged, though few have achieved an international reputation.

Traditional visual arts survive in works of tapestry, embroidery, leather, pottery, and ceramics, and in the manufacture of wool and goat-hair rugs with varicoloured stripes. Singing is also important, as is storytelling. Villagers have special songs for births, circumcisions, weddings, funerals, and harvesting. Several types of *dabkah* (group dances characterized by pounding feet on the floor to mark the rhythm) are danced on festive occasions, while the *sahjah* is a well-known Bedouin dance. The Circassian minority has a sword dance and several other Cossack dances. As part of its effort to preserve local performing arts, the government sponsors a national

Jordan plays host to major foreign film productions, such as Steven Spielberg's Indiana Jones and the Last Crusade, *starring Harrison Ford* (left) *and Sean Connery.* © Lucas Film LTD/Zuma Press

troupe that is regularly featured on state radio and television programs.

Jordan has a small film industry, and sites within the country, such as Petra and the Ramm valleys, have served as locations for major foreign productions, such as director David Lean's *Lawrence of Arabia* (1962) and Steven Spielberg's *Indiana Jones and the Last Crusade* (1989).

CULTURAL INSTITUTIONS

Jordan has numerous museums, particularly in Amman. The capital is home to museums dedicated to coins, geology, stamps, Islam, Jordanian folklore, and the military. The Jordan National Gallery of Fine Arts houses a collection of contemporary Arab and Muslim paintings as well as sculptures and ceramics. The ancient ruins at Petra, Qaṣr ʿAmrah, and Umm al-Rasass near Mādāba have all been designated UNESCO World Heritage sites. Additionally, several archaeological museums are located throughout the country.

SPORTS AND RECREATION

The most popular team sports in Jordan are football (soccer) and basketball, and handball and volleyball are also commonly played. In individual sports, boxing, tae kwon do, and swimming are the most widespread. Jordan has fielded teams for the Pan-Arab Games (Jordan hosted the event in 1999), the West Asian Games, and the Islamic Games. The participation of Jordanian athletes in various international competitions, notably those held in the Middle East, has encouraged better relations in the region. The country first competed in the Summer Olympic Games in 1984, but it has not participated in the Winter Games.

MEDIA AND PUBLISHING

Most newspapers, such as the English-language daily *Jordan Times*, are privately owned, but the government owns major shares in two of Jordan's largest dailies, *Al-Ra'y* ("The Opinion") and *Al-Dustour* ("The Constitution"). There are extensive press restrictions, and in 1998 a law was put into effect that further limited press freedoms. Since 2000, however, there has been an easing of some prohibitions. Jordan has several literary magazines, as well as scientific and topical periodicals. Radio and television stations, which are government-owned, feature programs from both Arab and Western countries.

CHAPTER 15

Jordan: Past and Present

Jordan occupies an area rich in archaeological remains and religious traditions. The Jordanian desert was home to hunters from the Lower Paleolithic Period, as evidenced by the wide distribution of their flint tools throughout the region. In the southeastern part of the country, at Mount Al-Ṭubayq, rock carvings date from several prehistoric periods, the earliest of which have been attributed to the Paleolithic-Mesolithic era. The site at Tulaylāt al-Ghassūl in the Jordan Valley of a well-built village with painted plaster walls may represent transitional developments from the Neolithic to the Chalcolithic period.

The Early Bronze Age (*c.* 3000–2100 BCE) is marked by deposits at the base of Dhībān. Although many sites have been found in the northern portion of the country, few have been excavated, and little evidence of settlement in this period is found south of Al-Shawbak. The region's early Bronze Age culture was terminated by a nomadic invasion that destroyed the principal towns and villages, marking the end of an apparently peaceful period of development. Security was not reestablished until the Egyptians arrived after 1580 BCE. It was once believed that the area was unoccupied from 1900 to 1300 BCE, but a systematic archaeological survey has shown that the country had a settled population throughout the period. This was confirmed by the discovery of a small temple at Amman with Egyptian, Mycenaean, and Cypriot imported objects.

BIBLICAL ASSOCIATIONS

Biblical accounts of the area, dating from the Middle Bronze Age onward, mention kingdoms such as Gilead in the north, Moab in central Jordan, and Midian in the south. At the time of the Exodus, the Israelites tried to pass through Edom in southern Jordan but were refused permission. They were at first repelled by the Amorites, whom they later defeated. The Israelite tribes of Gad and Reuben and half of the Manasseh group nonetheless settled in the conquered territory of the Ammonites, Amorites, and Bashan and rebuilt many of the towns they had partially destroyed. A record of this period is the Mesha (or Moabite) Stone found at Dhībān in 1868, now in the Louvre Museum in Paris. It is inscribed in an eastern form of Canaanite, closely akin to Hebrew.

The next few centuries (1300–1000 BCE) were marked by constant raiding from both sides of the Jordan River. David attacked and devastated Moab and Edom. Although held for a time, Ammon with its capital, Rabbath Ammon (modern Amman), regained independence on the death of David (*c.* 960 BCE). Solomon had a port on the Gulf of Aqaba at Ezion-geber (modern Elat, Israel), where copper ore was smelted from mines in the Wadi Al-ʿArabah and trade was carried on with the southern Arabian states. However, hostilities remained constant between Judah and Edom; a Hebrew king, Amaziah, even captured Sela (Petra), the capital.

The next invaders were the Assyrians, who under Adadnirari III (811/810–783 BCE) overran the eastern part of the country as far as Edom. Revolts against Assyrian rule occurred in the 760s and 750s, but the country was retaken in 734–733 by Tiglath-pileser III (ruled 745–727 BCE), who then devastated Israel, sent its people into exile, and divided the country into provinces under Assyrian governors. This policy of direct rule continued until the fall of the Assyrian empire in 612 BCE. The Assyrian texts are the first source to refer to the Nabataeans, who at this time occupied the land south and east of Edom (ancient Midian). After the fall of Assyria, the Moabites and Ammonites continued to raid Judah until the latter was conquered by the Neo-Babylonians under Nebuchadnezzar II. Little is known of the history of Jordan under the Neo-Babylonians and Persians, but during this period the Nabataeans infiltrated Edom and forced the Edomites into southern Palestine.

It was not until the Hellenistic rule of the Seleucids and the Ptolemies that the country prospered, trade increased, and new towns were built. Rabbath Ammon was renamed Philadelphia, and Jarash became Antioch-on-the-Chrysorrhoas, or Gerasa. Hostilities between the Seleucids and Ptolemies enabled the Nabataeans to extend their kingdom northward and to increase their prosperity based on the caravan trade with Arabia and Syria. The northern part of Jordan was for a time in Jewish hands, and there were constant struggles between the Jewish Maccabees and the Seleucids. Most of the Dead Sea Scrolls date from this period.

Ruins of the Roman city of Gerasa (foreground), *Jarash, Jordan.* Silvio Fiore/SuperStock, Inc.

During 64–63 BCE the kingdom of Nabataea was conquered by the Romans under Pompey, who restored the Hellenistic cities destroyed by the Jews and set up the Decapolis, a league of 10 ancient Greek cities. The country remained independent but paid imperial taxes. Roman policy seems to have been to maintain Nabataea as a buffer state against the desert tribes. In 25–24 BCE it served as a starting point for Aelius Gallus's ill-starred expedition in search of Arabia Felix. Nabataea was finally absorbed into the Roman Empire by Trajan in 105–106 CE as the province of Palaestina Tertia. Under Roman rule Jordan prospered, and many new towns and villages were established. The whole country, except the Decapolis, was made part of the new province called Arabia Petraea, with its capital first at Petra and later at Buṣrā al-Shām in Syria. After 313, Christianity became a recognized religion, and a large number of churches were built.

THE LATIN KINGDOM AND MUSLIM DOMINATION

The area was devastated in the 6th and 7th centuries by the intermittent warfare between Byzantium and Sāsānian Persia. In 627 the emperor Heraclius finally defeated the Persians and reestablished order, but Byzantium, gravely weakened by the long struggle, was unable to face the unexpected menace of a new power that had arisen in Arabia. In 636 the Muslims—led by the famous "Sword of Islam," Khālid ibn al-Walīd—destroyed a Byzantine army at the Battle of the Yarmūk River and brought the greater part of Syria and Palestine under Muslim rule.

The caliphs of the Umayyad dynasty (661–750) established their capital at Damascus and built hunting lodges and palaces in the Jordanian desert. These can still be seen at sites such as Qaṣr ʿAmrah, Al-Kharānah, Al-Ṭūbah, and

Petra

Petra (Arabic: Baṭrā) is an ancient city and the centre of an Arab kingdom in Hellenistic and Roman times. Its ruins are in southwest Jordan. The city was built on a terrace, pierced from east to west by the Wadi Mūsā (the Valley of Moses)—one of the places where, according to tradition, the Israelite leader Moses struck a rock and water gushed forth. The valley is enclosed by sandstone cliffs veined with shades of red and purple varying to pale yellow, and for this reason Petra was called by the 19th-century English biblical scholar John William Burgon a "rose-red city half as old as Time." The modern town of Wadi Mūsā, situated adjacent to the ancient city, chiefly serves the steady stream of tourists who continue to visit the site.

The Greek name Petra ("Rock") probably replaced the biblical name Sela. Remains from the Paleolithic and Neolithic periods have been discovered at Petra, and Edomites are known to have occupied the area about 1200 BCE. Centuries later the Nabataeans, an Arab tribe, occupied it and made it the capital of their kingdom. In 312 BCE the region was attacked by Seleucid forces, who failed to seize the city. Under Nabataean rule, Petra prospered as a centre of the spice trade that involved such disparate realms as China, Egypt, Greece, and India, and the city's population swelled to between 10,000 and 30,000.

When the Nabataeans were defeated by the Romans in 105–6 CE, Petra became part of the Roman province of Arabia but continued to flourish until changing trade routes caused its gradual commercial decline. After an earthquake (not the first) damaged the city in 551, significant habitation seems to have ceased. The Islamic invasion occurred in the 7th century, and a Crusader outpost is evidence of activity there in the 12th century. After the Crusades, the city was unknown to the Western world until it was rediscovered by the Swiss traveler Johann Ludwig Burckhardt in 1812.

Excavations from 1958 on behalf of the British School of Archaeology in Jerusalem and, later, the American Center of Oriental Research added greatly to knowledge of Petra. The ruins are usually approached from the east by a narrow gorge known as the Siq (Wadi Al-Sīq). Among the first sites viewed from the Siq is the Khaznah ("Treasury"), which is actually a large tomb. Al-Dayr ("the Monastery"), one of Petra's best-known rock-cut monuments, is an

The Nabataean rock-cut monument of Al-Dayr, Petra, Jordan. Brian Brake—Rapho/Photo Researchers

unfinished tomb facade that during Byzantine times was used as a church. Many of the tombs of Petra have elaborate facades and are now used as dwellings. The High Place of Sacrifice, a cultic altar dating from biblical times, is a well-preserved site. To support the ancient city's large population, its inhabitants maintained an extensive hydrological system, including dams, cisterns, rock-carved water channels, and ceramic pipes. Excavations begun in 1993 revealed several more temples and monuments that provide insight into the political, social, and religious traditions of the ancient city. The ruins are vulnerable to floods and other natural phenomena, and increased tourist traffic has also damaged the monuments. In 1985 Petra was designated a UNESCO World Heritage site.

Qaṣr al-Mushattā. Many Roman forts were also rebuilt. After the ʿAbbāsids seized power in 750, the capital was transferred to Baghdad, and Syria, which had been the Umayyad metropolitan province, was severely repressed.

Jordan, now distant from the centre of power, became a backwater and slowly returned to the old Bedouin way of life. With the capture of Jerusalem by the Crusaders in 1099, the Latin kingdom of Jerusalem was extended east of the Jordan, a principality known as Oultre Jourdain was established, and a capital was set up at Al-Karak. After the Crusaders retreated, the history of Jordan remained mostly uneventful. Not until the 16th century did it submit to Ottoman rule and become part of the *vilāyet* (province) of Damascus.

In the 19th century the Ottomans settled Circassian, Caucasian, and other refugees in Jordan to protect their communications with Arabia. Assisted by Germany, they completed in 1908 the Hejaz Railway linking Damascus and Medina.

TRANSJORDAN, THE HĀSHIMITE KINGDOM, AND THE PALESTINE WAR

During World War I the Arabs joined the British against the Ottomans. In a revolt of 1916, in which they were assisted by T. E. Lawrence (Lawrence of Arabia), the Arabs severed the Hejaz Railway. In July 1917 the army of Prince Fayṣal ibn Husayn (of the Hāshimite [or Hashemite] dynasty) captured Al-'Aqabah, and by October 1918 Amman and Damascus were in Allied hands. In 1920 the Conference of San Remo in Italy created two mandates: one, over Palestine, was given to Great Britain, and the other, over Syria and Lebanon, went to France. This act effectively separated the area now occupied by Israel and Jordan from that of Syria. In November 1920 'Abdullāh, Fayṣal's brother, arrived in Ma'ān (then part of the Hejaz) with 2,000 armed supporters intent on gathering together tribes to attack the French, who had forced Fayṣal to relinquish his newly founded kingdom in Syria. By April 1921, however, the British had decided that ʿAbdullāh would take over as ruler of what then became known as Transjordan.

Effectively, Turkish rule in Transjordan was simply replaced by British rule. The mandate, confirmed by the League of Nations in July 1922, gave the British virtually a free hand in administering the territory. However, in September, the establishment of "a Jewish national home" was explicitly excluded from the mandate's clauses, and it was made clear that the area would also be closed to Jewish immigration. On May 25, 1923, the British recognized Transjordan's independence under the rule of Emir ʿAbdullāh, but, as outlined in a treaty as well as the constitution in 1928, matters of finance, military, and foreign affairs would remain in the hands of a British "resident." Full independence was finally achieved after World War II by a treaty concluded in London on March 22, 1946, and ʿAbdullāh subsequently proclaimed himself king. A new constitution was promulgated, and in 1949 the name of the state was changed to the Hāshimite Kingdom of Jordan.

Throughout the interwar years ʿAbdullāh had depended on British financial support. The British also assisted him in forming an elite force called the Arab Legion, comprising Bedouin troops but under the command of and trained by British officers, which was used to maintain and secure the allegiance of ʿAbdullāh's Bedouin subjects. On May 15, 1948, the day after the Jewish Agency proclaimed the independent state of Israel and immediately following the British withdrawal from Palestine, Transjordan joined its Arab neighbours in the first Arab-Israeli war. The Arab Legion, commanded by Glubb Pasha (John [later Sir John] Bagot Glubb), and Egyptian, Syrian, Lebanese, and Iraqi troops entered Palestine. ʿAbdullāh's primary purpose, which he had spelled out in secret discussions with

Hāshimite

Hāshimites are the Arab descendants, either direct or collateral, of the prophet Muhammad, from among whom came the family that created the 20th-century Hāshimite dynasty. Muhammad himself was a member of the house of Hāshim, a subdivision of the Quraysh tribe. The most revered line of Hāshimites passed through Ḥasan, son of the Prophet's daughter Fāṭimah and her husband, ʿAlī, the fourth caliph. Ḥasan was the last of this line to hold disputed claim to the caliphate, but his progeny eventually established themselves as hereditary emirs of Mecca, the role continuing under Ottoman rule. Of such lineage were Ḥusayn ibn ʿAlī, emir of Mecca and king of Hejaz from 1916 to 1924, and his sons Fayṣal and ʿAbdullāh, who became kings of Iraq and Jordan, respectively, founding the modern Hāshimite dynasty.

Jewish envoys, was to extend his rule to include the area allotted to the Palestinian Arabs under the UN partition resolution of November 1947. Accordingly, he engaged his forces in the region of Palestine now popularly known as the West Bank (the area just west of the Jordan River) and expelled Jewish forces from East Jerusalem (the Old City). When the Jordan-Israel armistice was signed on April 3, 1949, the West Bank and East Jerusalem—an area of about 2,100 square miles (5,400 square km)—came under Jordanian rule, and almost half a million Palestinian Arabs joined the half million Transjordanians. One year later, Jordan formally annexed this territory. Israel and Britain had tacitly agreed to ʿAbdullāh keeping the area, but the Arab countries and most of the world opposed the king's action. Only Britain and Pakistan recognized the annexation. The incorporation into Jordan of the West Bank Palestinians and a large refugee population that was hostile to the Hāshimite regime brought severe economic and political consequences. Conversely, ʿAbdullāh gained such

deter these operations. Relations between Jordan and Syria and Egypt and between the Palestinians and Jordan soon deteriorated. Ḥussein continued private talks with Israel over the internal and external dangers both countries faced. In late 1966 the Israeli army made a devastating raid into the West Bank village of Al-Samū' south of Hebron. Ḥussein responded by attempting to stop the passage of Syrian-based Palestinian guerrillas coming through Jordan into Israel, and he eventually broke off diplomatic ties with Syria. However, as tension mounted between Israel and Egypt and Syria in the spring of 1967, Jordan reversed its position and signed a defense pact with Egypt and Syria. Israeli and Jordanian forces clashed in East Jerusalem, and in June 1967 Ḥussein joined Egypt and Syria in the third Arab-Israeli war.

The June 1967 war was a watershed in the modern history of Jordan. Within 48 hours Israeli forces had overrun the entire territory west of the Jordan River, capturing Bethlehem, Hebron, Jericho, Nāblus, Ramallah, Janīn, and the city of Jerusalem. Jordan suffered heavy casualties and lost one-third of its most fertile land. Its already overburdened economy was then faced with supporting tens of thousands of new refugees. Ḥussein had regarded entering the war as the lesser of two evils: he believed that if he had not joined Egypt and Syria, they would have supported the Palestinians in overthrowing his regime. The loss of the West Bank and Jerusalem, devastating as it was, was preferable to the loss of his kingdom.

From 1967 to Civil War

Following the June War, Ḥussein faced three major problems: how to recover from the economic losses caused by the war, how to live with Israel's occupation of the West Bank and the annexation of East Jerusalem, and how to preserve the Hāshimite throne against a considerably augmented and increasingly hostile Palestinian population. The war reversed the progress made in Jordan's economy prior to June 1967, even with financial aid from Saudi Arabia, Kuwait, and Libya. Yet within a short period both the United States and Great Britain resumed economic and military aid, which helped to restore its economy and to preserve peace. In 1971 arrangements were also made with Israel enabling Jordanians to farm in the Jordan Valley.

In spite of the fact that an Arab summit meeting held in Khartoum, Sudan, in August 1967 passed the "three noes" resolution—no peace with Israel, no recognition of Israel, and no negotiations with Israel—Ḥussein resumed his secret negotiations with Israel over the disposition of the West Bank and East Jerusalem. Relations with Israel were thus inseparably linked to the future of the Palestinians. Ḥussein sought the return of all the lost territory but still privately recognized Israel and cooperated with it across a wide range of issues. Even so, he was not prepared to sign a peace treaty with the Jewish state. The two countries were thus no longer enemies and worked together against PLO terrorism, but little progress was made toward a lasting peace.

Ḥussein's relations with the PLO, which under the chairmanship of Yāsir ʿArafāt openly challenged the king's control in East Jordan, reached a crisis in September 1970. The Popular Front for the Liberation of Palestine (PFLP), a radical Marxist Palestinian group, hijacked four international airliners and blew up three of them in Dawson's Field, a deserted airstrip in the Jordanian desert. Ḥussein declared martial law, and civil war (later remembered as Black September) erupted. When 250 Syrian tanks entered northern Jordan in support of the PLO, Ḥussein was forced not only to call upon military assistance from the United States and Great Britain but also to allow overflights by

Israel to attack the Syrian forces. The Syrian forces were defeated, and a peace agreement, in which Ḥussein made concessions to the PLO, was signed by Ḥussein and 'Arafāt in Cairo on September 27, 1970. By July 1971, Ḥussein had forced the PLO guerrillas out of Jordan.

From 1973 to the Intifāḍah

Ḥussein chose not to join Egypt and Syria in their surprise attack on Israel in October 1973, although he did make a symbolic gesture by sending tanks to assist Syria in the Golan Heights. In negotiations immediately following the war, Ḥussein once again demanded the return of the West Bank and East Jerusalem from Israel. He was bitter that Israel—in response to pressure from U.S. Secretary of State Henry Kissinger—proposed a withdrawal of its forces from Israeli-occupied Egyptian territory but made no such overtures to Jordan. However, by August 1974 discussions were under way with Israel over "disengagement accords," which recognized Jordan as the speaker for the Palestinians and encouraged regional economic and tactical cooperation, especially in relation to the threat posed by Palestinian guerrilla groups. In October leaders of the Arab League at an Arab summit meeting in Rabat, Morocco, declared that the Palestinian people, under the leadership of the PLO ("their sole legitimate representative"), had the right to establish a national independent authority in liberated Palestine. In response Ḥussein announced that his country would exclude the West Bank from Jordan and would never enter into a federation with a Palestinian state, as such a step would inevitably give the Palestinian population a majority and bring about the loss of his kingdom.

Faced with American reluctance to supply arms and an Egyptian-Israeli Sinai accord, Jordan with Syria agreed in August 1975 to form a joint "supreme command" to coordinate their foreign and military policies in an effort to control PLO activities. In March 1977 Ḥussein met with 'Arafāt in Cairo, their first meeting since Black September in 1970. In July 1977 Ḥussein, Egyptian president Anwar el-Sādāt, and U.S. president Jimmy Carter once again discussed the possibility of a link between Jordan and a Palestinian "entity," but it was denounced by the PLO.

The election of the right-wing Likud bloc in Israel with Menachem Begin as prime minister in May 1977 brought relations between Jordan and Israel to a low ebb. Determined to annex and retain all of the West Bank, which Israel now called Judaea and Samaria, Begin greatly accelerated the program of constructing Jewish settlements in the West Bank and Gaza. Under the terms of the Camp David Accords in 1978, Israel committed itself to granting autonomy to the Palestinians and to negotiating the future status of the occupied territories, but Ḥussein condemned the agreement and completely broke off the 15-year secret negotiations with Israel. From late 1977 until 1984, Jordanian contacts with Israel essentially came to a halt. Ḥussein became increasingly alarmed at the growing popularity in Israel of the view that Jordan was, in fact, the Palestinian state, which would also resolve the conflict between Israel and the Palestinians. Israel's invasion of Lebanon in 1982 fueled fears in Amman that the first step in the process of transferring Palestinians to the East Bank was under way.

In the early 1980s Ḥussein sought an accommodation with 'Arafāt and the PLO after the PLO had been expelled from Lebanon and its bases had been destroyed. The two men reached a temporary and somewhat uneasy alliance. To strengthen his legitimacy in the eyes of Palestinians, in 1984 Ḥussein allowed the Palestine National Council (a virtual parliament of the Palestinians) to meet in Amman. In February 1985 he signed an agreement with 'Arafāt pledging cooperation with the PLO and coordination of a joint peace initiative. Ḥussein believed that ʿArafāt would accept a confederation of the West and East Banks with autonomy for the Palestinians of the West Bank under Jordanian sovereignty. ʿArafāt, however, had not given up hope of an independent Palestinian state in the West Bank, although he was agreeable to an eventual confederation between such a future Palestinian state and Jordan.

In February 1986 Ḥussein, frustrated by ʿArafāt's ambiguity regarding the PLO's recognition of Israel and renunciation of terrorism, repudiated the Amman agreement with ʿArafāt and broke off negotiations with the PLO. Although the king was careful not to expel the PLO from Jordan entirely, in spite of an increase in guerrilla violence in the West Bank, he did order the closure of the PLO offices in Amman. In a complete turnaround in the Jordanian policy that had been followed since the Arab summit at Rabat in 1974, Ḥussein declared that he would now be responsible for the economic welfare of the West Bank Palestinians. In addition, the king announced that the West Bank would be included in an upcoming five-year plan for Jordan and approved an increase in the number of Palestinian seats (to about half) in an enlarged National Assembly. His goal was to create a Jordanian-Palestinian-Israeli administration that would make the West Bank independent of the PLO and enable him to reach a settlement with Israel, in which he would regain at least partial sovereignty of the area.

By April 1987 Ḥussein and Shimon Peres, then Israel's foreign minister, had agreed to a UN-sponsored conference involving all parties to seek a comprehensive peace. Palestinian representatives would be part of a Jordanian-Palestinian delegation. Although the proposal was endorsed by U.S. president Ronald Reagan, Israeli prime minister Yitzhak Shamir wanted a conference with only Jordan and resisted U.S. pressure for a comprehensive peace conference. Ḥussein scored a diplomatic triumph by staging an Arab League summit meeting in Amman in November, during which league members agreed to reestablish diplomatic relations with Egypt that had been severed following the Camp David Accords. More importantly for Ḥussein, the Palestinian issue was not the main topic. Instead, the Iran-Iraq War, then in its eighth year, took precedence.

The situation changed dramatically in December, however, with the outbreak of the *intifāḍah*, a Palestinian uprising on the West Bank. Ḥussein quickly realized that the uprising was directed against his rule as well as that of the Israelis. His immediate response was to support the *intifāḍah* publicly and to offer aid to families of victims of Israeli reprisals in an effort to deflect the hostility toward his regime. But the *intifāḍah* leaders (known as the Unified Command) renounced the king's overtures, and ʿArafāt quickly assumed the role of spokesman for the revolt. The *intifāḍah* brought to a halt Jordanian and Israeli plans for an economic path to peace. Ḥussein thus canceled the five-year plan for the West Bank.

Renouncing Claims to the West Bank

An emergency meeting of the Arab League in June 1988 gave the PLO financial control of support for the Palestinians, thereby virtually acknowledging ʿArafāt as their spokesman. In response, Ḥussein renounced all Jordanian claims to the West Bank, allowing the PLO to assume full responsibility there. He dissolved the Jordanian parliament (half of whose members were West Bank representatives), ceased salary payments to 21,000 West Bank civil servants, and ordered that West Bank Palestinian passports be converted to two-year travel documents. When the Palestine

National Council recognized the PLO as the sole legal representative of the Palestinian people and proclaimed the independence of a purely notional Palestine on November 15, 1988, Ḥussein immediately extended recognition to the Palestinian entity.

In November 1989 Jordan held its first parliamentary elections in 22 years. Opposition groups, particularly the fundamentalist Muslim Brotherhood—in the form of the Islamic Action Front (IAF)—gained more seats than the pro-government candidates, and the newly elected prime minister, Mudar Badran, promised to lift the martial law that had been in place since 1967—a promise not fully kept until July 1991.

From the Persian Gulf War to Peace with Israel

Iraq's invasion of Kuwait in August 1990 and the subsequent Persian Gulf War forced Ḥussein to choose between two allies, the United States and Iraq. The king leaned heavily toward Iraqi leader Ṣaddām Ḥussein, who also received a zealous and vocal groundswell of support from the Jordanian people. In addition, trade with Iraq represented two-fifths of the kingdom's GDP. Kuwait's allies immediately cut off all aid to Jordan, imposed an air and sea blockade, and condemned King Ḥussein's actions. To make matters worse, between 200,000 and 300,000 refugees from Kuwait were expelled or fled (back) to Jordan. However, by the end of 1991 the United States and Israel were again seeking Ḥussein's support for an American-Israeli peace initiative.

The first multiparty general election since 1956 was scheduled for November 1993. In August the king dissolved the 80-member House of Representatives (the lower house of the National Assembly) and announced that the election would be conducted on a one-person-one-vote system rather than on the old "slate" system that allowed voters to cast as many votes as there were representatives in their constituency. In the election the number of seats won by anti-Zionist Islamic militants—who made up the IAF, a coalition of Islamic groupings and the largest of Jordan's political parties—was reduced from 36 to 16, which gave the king the support he needed to carry out his policy.

Ḥussein expressed public reservations over a PLO-Israeli accord in 1993 but nonetheless stated his willingness to support the Palestinian people. He was concerned over issues relating to Jordan's economic links with the West Bank and the future status of Palestinians in Jordan. About a year later, Jordan and Israel signed a peace treaty in which Ḥussein was recognized as the custodian of the Muslim holy sites in East Jerusalem.

Ḥussein's Last Years and the Ascension of 'Abdullāh II

In January 1995 Ḥussein signed accords with the PLO pledging support for Palestinian autonomy and the establishment of a Palestinian state that included East Jerusalem. The Palestinians nevertheless remained hostile to the peace treaty with Israel, as did Syria and a large segment of the population led by the IAF. Ḥussein became increasingly frustrated with what he considered to be the obstructionist policies of the Israeli government, but he still played a central role in brokering a deal between Israel and the PLO regarding Israeli withdrawal from Hebron in the West Bank in early 1997. In addition, Ḥussein acted as a mediator between the Israelis and Palestinians in an agreement made in October 1998 at the Wye Plantation in eastern Maryland.

By then Ḥussein's health was failing. Shortly before his death in February 1999, he proclaimed his son ʿAbdullāh to be his successor, rather than his brother Hassan (Ḥasan), who had been the crown prince. In the main, King ʿAbdullāh II continued to carry out his father's policies and maintained that the new government he formed in March would focus on integrating economic reforms, bettering Jordan's relations with its Arab neighbours, and improving the status of women. The king faced numerous problems, however, including a growing tide of domestic dissent over the country's close ties with the United States and its continued diplomatic relations with Israel.

In subsequent years, the new monarch carved out a vigorous foreign policy that generally reflected his original goals. Strong political and economic bonds were formed with neighbouring Arab states—especially Egypt and Syria—and the king reshuffled his cabinet on several occasions while attempting to modernize and invigorate the economy. Government security services thwarted several violent attacks by Islamic militants (directed mostly at the security services themselves), and parliamentary elections took place in 2003. The new parliament was made up mostly of independents, but the IAF polled highest among the organized parties.

CONCLUSION

At the end of the first decade of the 21st century, Syria continued to be under the authoritarian rule of the ʿAlawite al-Assad family. Bashar al-Assad, president since 2000, remained firmly at the helm, meaning that Syria had been governed by only two leaders—a father and his son—for four decades. Syrian relations with the West, and especially with the United States, were sometimes troubled, particularly given U.S. allegations that Syria supported terrorism and harboured questionable nuclear ambitions. Syrian-Lebanese relations also remained an issue of regional import, and in 2008 Syria and Lebanon established diplomatic relations for the first time.

Although its massively devastating civil war had been over for some two decades, Lebanon continued to face entrenched political difficulties and periodic violence. Competition for influence in the political sphere included efforts by Hezbollah, which obtained a controversial veto power in the Lebanese parliament. Continued interference in Lebanese politics by external actors, especially Syria, continued to confound a normalized political environment. Warfare between Hezbollah and Israel periodically brought renewed violence to Lebanon.

The question of Jordan's large Palestinian population remained a central issue in Jordanian politics, and the Hāshimite regime continued to demonstrate that progress of Arab-Israeli peace talks was a key interest. Long-standing concern that Jordan might be considered an alternative Palestinian homeland remained a source of acute distress for the Jordanian leadership. Jordan continued to maintain a generally positive relationship with the West, and its peace treaty with Israel was one of the most secure among the Arab states.

As neighbours, the fortunes of Syria, Lebanon, and Jordan have interlocked to varying degrees: hegemony in Lebanon has long been a Syrian priority, while Jordan's close relations with Iraq and its peace agreement with Israel have in turn historically meant difficult relations with Syria. Although Jordan and Lebanon do not share a border, Jordan has made it clear that a stable Lebanon is in Jordan's best interests. At the end of the first decade of the 21st century, the relationships between Syria, Lebanon, and Jordan—and their relations with Israel, the wider region, and the international community—continued to evolve.

GLOSSARY

annexation The incorporation of a territory or nation into an existing nation or state.

bicameral system System of government in which the legislature comprises two houses.

caliph A leader who serves as the successor of Muhammad as temporal and spiritual head of Islam.

cassation The act of annulling, cancelling, or quashing.

cavalry Military force mounted on horseback, formerly an important element in the armies of all major powers.

conscript To enroll into service by compulsion; to draft.

coup d'état The violent overthrow or alteration of an existing government by a small group.

court of cassation The highest court of appeal.

desalination Removal of dissolved salts from seawater and from the salty waters of inland seas, highly mineralized groundwaters, and municipal wastewaters.

Druze Relatively small Middle Eastern religious sect.

envoy Any person deputed to represent one sovereign or government in its intercourse with another.

fresco painting Method of wall painting in which water-based pigments are applied to wet, freshly laid lime plaster.

garrison A military post; especially a permanent military installation.

guerrilla Member of an irregular military force fighting small-scale, fast-moving actions, usually in concert with an overall political-military strategy, against conventional military and police forces.

hegemony Leadership or predominant influence exercised by one power over another.

intifāḍah Uprising or rebellion; specifically an armed uprising of Palestinians against Israeli occupation of the West Bank and Gaza Strip.

Janissaries Elite corps of the Ottoman Empire's army from the late 14th to the early 19th century.

khamsin Hot, dry, dusty wind in North Africa and the Arabian Peninsula that blows from the south or southeast in late winter and early spring.

marl Earthy mixture of fine-grained minerals that range widely in composition.

Maronite Church Eastern-rite community of the Roman Catholic church centred in Lebanon (Eastern Rite Church).

Monothelite Any of the 7th-century Christians who, while otherwise orthodox, maintained that Christ had only one will.

necropolis (Greek: "city of the dead") Extensive and elaborate burial place serving an ancient city.

pantheon All the gods of a people considered as a group.

particularism A political theory or practice advocating a right and freedom for each politically conscious or organized group to promote its own interests and especially independence.

promulgate To declare; to set forth publicly.

suffete One of the two annually elected chief magistrates of ancient Carthage.

Sufism Mystical movement within Islam that seeks to find divine love and knowledge through direct personal experience of God.

suzerain A dominant state exercising political control over a dependent state.

tunny Tuna; especially bluefin.

BIBLIOGRAPHY

Syria is discussed in its geographic context in Peter Mansfield, *The Middle East: A Political and Economic Survey*, 5th ed. (1980). Thomas Collelo (ed.), *Syria, a Country Study*, 3rd ed. (1988) is a more specific study. Andrea B. Rugh, *Within the Circle: Parents and Children in an Arab Village* (1997), studies family life in contemporary Syria.

Thomas Collelo (ed.), *Syria, a Country Study*, 3rd ed. (1988), includes a historical overview. Studies of Syria's ancient history are found in *The Cambridge Ancient History* (1923–), especially volumes 1–4 and 6–7, some in later 2nd and 3rd editions; Lisa Cooper, *Early Urbanism on the Syrian Euphrates* (2006); Paolo Matthiae, *Ebla: An Empire Rediscovered* (1980; originally published in Italian, 1977); J. Perrot, A. Kempinski, and M. Avi-Yonah, *Syria-Palestine*, 2 vol. (1979; originally published in French, 1978–80); Glanville Downey, *A History of Antioch in Syria: From Seleucus to the Arab Conquest* (1961); A. H. M. Jones, *The Cities of the Eastern Roman Provinces*, 2nd ed., rev. by M. Avi-Yonah (1971, reissued 1983), chapter 10; and F. M. Heichelheim, "Roman Syria," in Tenney Frank (ed.), *An Economic Survey of Ancient Rome*, vol. 4 (1938, reprinted 1975), pp. 121–257.

The medieval period is covered in such general histories as Philip K. Hitti, *History of Syria*, 2nd ed. (1957); and in the more-specialized works Hugh Kennedy, *The Byzantine and Early Islamic Near East* (2006); Paul M. Cobb, *White Banners: Contention in 'Abbāsid Syria, 750–880* (2001); and R. Stephen Humphreys, *From Saladin to the Mongols: The Ayyubids of Damascus, 1193–1260* (1977). Ottoman Syria's early political history is outlined in detail in Abdul-Rahim Abu-Husayn, *Provincial Leaderships in Syria, 1575–1650* (1985). Later periods are dealt with in James Grehan, *Everyday Life & Consumer Culture in 18th-Century Damascus*

(2007); Karl K. Barbir, *Ottoman Rule in Damascus, 1708–1758* (1980); and Abraham Marcus, *The Middle East on the Eve of Modernity: Aleppo in the Eighteenth Century* (1989).

General studies concentrating on modern history include Derek Hopwood, *Syria 1945–1986: Politics and Society* (1988); and A. H. Hourani, *Syria and Lebanon* (1946, reprinted 1968). More particular aspects of Syria's modern history and politics are covered by Hanna Batatu, *Syria's Peasantry, the Descendants of Its Lesser Rural Notables, and Their Politics* (1999); Steven Heydemann, *Authoritarianism in Syria: Institutions and Social Conflict, 1946–1970* (1999); James L. Gelvin, *Divided Loyalties: Nationalism and Mass Politics in Syria at the Close of Empire* (1998); Volker Perthes, *The Political Economy of Syria Under Assad* (1995); Raymond A. Hinnebusch, *Authoritarian Power and State Formation in Ba'thist Syria: Army, Party, and Peasant* (1990); Patrick Seale, *Asad of Syria: The Struggle for the Middle East* (1989); Philip S. Khoury, *Syria and the French Mandate: The Politics of Arab Nationalism, 1920–1945* (1987); Lisa Wedeen, *Ambiguities of Domination: Politics, Rhetoric, and Symbols in Contemporary Syria* (1999), and Annabelle Böttcher, *Official Sunni and Shi'i Islam in Syria* (2002).

General discussions of the Lebanese land and people may be found in David C. Gordon, *The Republic of Lebanon: Nation in Jeopardy* (1983). Economic and social matters are discussed in World Bank, *Lebanon Private Sector Assessment* (1995); Salim Nasr, "New Social Realities and Post-War Lebanon: Issues for Reconstruction," in Philip S. Khoury and Samir Khalaf (eds.), *Recovering Beirut* (1993), pp. 63–80; Huda C. Zurayk and Haroutune K. Armenian, *Beirut 1984* (1985); Abdul-Amir Badrud-din, *The Bank of Lebanon* (1984); Friedrich Ragette (ed.), *Beirut of Tomorrow: Planning for Reconstruction* (1983); Joseph Chamie, *Religion and Fertility: Arab Christian-Muslim Differentials* (1981);

Nadim G. Khalaf, *The Economic Implications of the Size of Nations, with Special Reference to Lebanon* (1971).

Useful discussions of Lebanese government include Guilain Denoeux and Robert Springborg, "Hariri's Lebanon," *Middle East Policy*, 6(2):158–73 (October 1998); William W. Harris, *Faces of Lebanon: Sects, Wars, and Global Extensions* (1997); Charles Winslow, *Lebanon: War and Politics in a Fragmented Society* (1996); R. D. McLaurin, "Lebanon and Its Army: Past, Present, and Future," in Edward E. Azar et al., *The Emergence of a New Lebanon: Fantasy or Reality?* (1984), pp. 79–114; and Michael W. Suleiman, *Political Parties in Lebanon: The Challenge of a Fragmented Political Culture* (1967).

Cultural matters in Lebanon are discussed by Lawrence I. Conrad, "Culture and Learning in Beirut," *The American Scholar*, 52:463–478 (Autumn 1983); and Friedrich Ragette, *Architecture in Lebanon: The Lebanese House During the 18th and 19th Centuries* (1974, reprinted 1980).

Lebanon's ancient history is detailed in *The Cambridge Ancient History*, especially vol. 1 in 2 parts, 3rd ed. (1970–71), vol. 2, part 1, 3rd ed. (1973), and vol. 3, part 3, 2nd ed. (1982); and in Donald Harden, *The Phoenicians*, rev. ed. (1971). Other useful studies include Maurice Dunand, *Byblos: Its History, Ruins, and Legends*, 2nd ed. (1968; originally published in French, 2nd ed., 1968); Friedrich Ragette, *Baalbek* (1980); F. M. Heichelheim, "Roman Syria," in Tenney Frank (ed.), *An Economic Survey of Ancient Rome*, vol. 4 (1938, reprinted 1975), pp. 121–257; and Nina Jidejian, *Byblos Through the Ages* (1968), *Tyre Through the Ages* (1969), *Sidon Through the Ages* (1971), *Beirut Through the Ages* (1973), and *Baalbek: Heliopolis, City of the Sun* (1975).

The most important works on Lebanon's medieval and modern history include Philip K. Hitti, *Lebanon in History: From the Earliest Times to the Present*, 3rd ed. (1967); and Kamal

S. Salibi, *The Modern History of Lebanon* (1965, reissued 1977), and *A House of Many Mansions: The History of Lebanon Reconsidered* (1988). The Ottoman period is discussed by Abdul-Rahim Abu-Husayn, *Provincial Leaderships in Syria, 1575–1650* (1985); and Iliya F. Harik, *Politics and Change in a Traditional Society: Lebanon, 1711–1845* (1968).

The 20th-century history of Lebanon is explored by Michael C. Hudson, *The Precarious Republic: Political Modernization in Lebanon* (1968, reissued 1985). The civil war and subsequent events are evaluated by Kamal S. Salibi, *Cross Roads to Civil War: Lebanon, 1958–1976* (1976, reissued as *Crossroads to Civil War*, 1988); Walid Khalidi, "Lebanon: Yesterday and Tomorrow," *The Middle East Journal*, 43(3):375–387 (Summer 1989); Helena Cobban, *The Making of Modern Lebanon* (1985); David Gilmour, *Lebanon, the Fractured Country*, rev. and updated ed. (1987); N. Kliot, "The Collapse of the Lebanese State," *Middle Eastern Studies*, 23(1):54–74 (January 1987); Halim Barakat (ed.), *Toward a Viable Lebanon* (1988); Augustus Richard Norton and Jillian Schwedler, "Swiss Soldiers, Ta'if Clocks, and Early Elections: Toward a Happy Ending?" in Deirdre Collings (ed.), *Peace for Lebanon?: From War to Reconstruction* (1994), pp. 45–68; Rosemary Hollis and Nadim Shehadi (eds.), *Lebanon on Hold: Implications for Middle East Peace* (1996); Elizabeth Picard, *Lebanon: A Shattered Country*, rev. ed. (2002; originally published in French, 1988); and Habib C. Malik, *Between Damascus and Jerusalem: Lebanon and Middle East Peace*, updated ed. (2000).

Overviews of all aspects of Jordan include Raphael Patai, *The Kingdom of Jordan* (1958, reprinted 1984); Helen Chapin Metz (ed.), *Jordan: A Country Study*, 4th ed. (1991); and Peter Gubser, *Jordan: Crossroads of Middle Eastern Events* (1983). Further resources may be found in Ian J. Seccombe (compiler), *Jordan* (1984), an annotated bibliography; and the bibliography in Peter Gubser, *Historical Dictionary of the Hashemite Kingdom of Jordan* (1991).

Colbert C. Held and Mildred McDonald Held, *Middle East Patterns: Places, Peoples, and Politics*, 2nd ed. (1994), places Jordan in a larger context. Rami G. Khouri, *The Jordan Valley: Life and Society Below Sea Level* (1981, reissued 1988), addresses agriculture and development on both sides of the river. Christine Osborne, *An Insight and Guide to Jordan* (1981), offers an overview of the landscape, society, and culture. Gerald Sparrow, *Modern Jordan* (1961), recounts the author's travels. A. H. Hourani, *Minorities in the Arab World* (1947, reprinted 1982), is a scholarly account of the various minority groups and their backgrounds. Studies in social anthropology include Richard T. Antoun, *Arab Village: A Social Structural Study of a Transjordanian Peasant Community* (1972, reissued 1977); Peter Gubser, *Politics and Change in Al-Karak, Jordan: A Study of a Small Arab Town and Its District* (1973, reissued 1985); and Paul A. Jureidini and R. D. McLaurin, *Jordan: The Impact of Social Change on the Role of the Tribes* (1984). Shelagh Weir, *The Bedouin*, new ed. (1990), provides an illustrated study of the arts and crafts of the Bedouin of Jordan. Norman N. Lewis, *Nomads and Settlers in Syria and Jordan, 1800–1980* (1987), traces the shift from a grazing economy to a sedentary agricultural society. Economic and political conditions are addressed in Michael P. Mazur, *Economic Growth and Development in Jordan* (1979); Bichara Khader and Adnan Badran (eds.), *The Economic Development of Jordan* (1987), a collection of essays; Naseer H. Aruri, *Jordan: A Study in Political Development (1921–1965)* (1972); and Rodney Wilson (ed.), *Politics and the Economy in Jordan* (1991).

The history of Jordan within the region is studied in William L. Cleveland, *A History of the Modern Middle East*, 2nd ed. (1999); and Arthur Goldschmidt Jr., *A Concise*

History of the Middle East, 6th ed. (1999). The most accessible general study of Jordanian history is Kamal Salibi, *The Modern History of Jordan* (1993, reissued 1998). Adnan Hadidi (ed.), *Studies in the History and Archaeology of Jordan*, 3 vol. (1982–87), contains detailed analyses of ancient and medieval history. Mary C. Wilson, *King Abdullah, Britain, and the Making of Jordan* (1987, reissued 1990); and Avi Shlaim, *Collusion Across the Jordan: King Abdullah, the Zionist Movement, and the Partition of Palestine* (1988), also available in rev. abridged ed., *The Politics of Partition* (1998), examine the role of King Abdullah at critical points in Jordan's history. Amnon Cohen, *Political Parties in the West Bank Under the Jordanian Regime, 1949–1967*, (1982, originally published in Hebrew, 1980); Shaul Mishal, *West Bank/East Bank: The Palestinians in Jordan, 1949–1967* (1978); and Clinton Bailey, *Jordan's Palestinian Challenge, 1948–1983: A Political History* (1984), discuss Jordan and the Palestinians. P. J. Vatikiotis, *Politics and the Military in Jordan: A Study of the Arab Legion, 1921–1957* (1967), outlines the historical influence of the military on Jordanian politics. Valerie Yorke, *Domestic Politics and Regional Security: Jordan, Syria, and Israel* (1988), examines Jordan's domestic political dynamics. Madiha Rashid Al Madfai, *Jordan, the United States, and the Middle East Peace Process, 1974–1991* (1993), explores Jordan's diplomatic role.

INDEX

A

B

E

F

G

H

K

L

M